Sacred Seasons

Sacred Seasons

A Journey through the Church Year

Brett Webb-Mitchell
and Diane Archer

The Pilgrim Press
Cleveland

To Adrianne and Parker Webb-Mitchell and Bryan Archer

And all the generations who have taught us and will
Teach others the beautiful stories found in the treasure chest
Of holidays of the church year.

The Pilgrim Press, 700 Prospect Avenue East
Cleveland, Ohio 44115-1100
pilgrimpress.com

Printed in the United States of America on acid-free paper

07 06 05 04 03 02 5 4 3 2 1

Library of Congress Cataloging-in-Publication Data

Webb-Mitchell, Brett.
Sacred seasons : a journey through the church year / Brett Webb-Mitchell and Diane Archer.
p. cm.
Includes bibliographical references.
ISBN 0-8298-1474-4 (alk. paper)
1. Church year—Study and teaching. I. Archer, Diane, 1956- II. Title.

BV30 .W38 2002
263'.9—dc21

2002022904

Contents

Preface

For many years, one of the tasks often done in my classes at Duke University's Divinity School was naming the many ways that the life of the church determines all aspects of our life together as Christians. For example, how does the church's calendar, or more precisely, the days of the church year, shape our Christian lives? We talk about the beginning of the church year commencing with the first Sunday of Advent, which is not the same as the larger society's understanding of January 1 as the first day of the new year. So how does celebrating the days of the church year guide our scattered lives into the common life discovered in the unity of the body of Christ? And what effect does knowing and practicing the holy days of the church calendar have on the rhythm of our life in our congregations and parishes?

One year, a group of students was particularly intrigued by these questions and decided to work with me on the project of educating churches in the ways of the church year. During our work together, we realized that there were common, distracting experiences that we shared. For example, while we all shared an occasional Advent wreath-lighting service in worship, we were struck by how the joyous festivities of Christmas disrupted the tail end of Advent and left nothing after Christmas itself but a lost sense of the importance of Epiphany. And what is a "Shrove Tuesday" or "Mardi Gras," and why is Lent forty days? What does it mean to celebrate Easter not for just a day, but for fifty days or more if we put Easter in the middle of Ash Wednesday and Pentecost Sunday? Or who ever celebrated All Hallows' Eve? We realized that we were uneducated, miseducated, or undereducated about the church calendar in our Protestant Church's upbringing. Furthermore, on closer examination, numerous people who are Roman Catholic practice the celebration of many of these days of the church calendar but are not quite sure of the origin or the purpose of the celebratory days.

What is a group of educators in the church to do?

Our response is *Sacred Seasons.*

The goal of *Sacred Seasons* is to teach congregations and parishes, Catholic and Protestant alike, the rich stories that illustrate the wondrous yet extraordinarily complex and symbol-filled practices of certain days in the church calendar, so that our lives may be ordered by the rhythm of life in Christ's body. For example, we begin *Sacred Seasons* with the first Sunday of Advent, which is the beginning of the church year for many of our churches. In a way, the first Sunday of Advent is our New Year's Day as Christians as the end of the church year, Christ the King Sunday or the Reign of Christ, is our New Year's Eve day. It just so happens to fall on or around the day known as Thanksgiving (in the United States) rather than January 1.

Writing *Sacred Seasons* is also in response to the increasing interest among many mainline Protestant congregations, and even some Roman Catholic parishes, in celebrating the days of great significance in the life of the church. Usually, these days are named and celebrated—even in a cursory manner—in the context of a congregation's worship. However, what has been weak or missing among the members of many congregations or parishes is a basic understanding of what the day actually signifies or embodies in terms of Christ's life and the life of the church. Furthermore, many people have little-to-no knowledge of the origin of some Christian traditions, many of which are pagan in nature. *Sacred Seasons* is not meant to replace worship, but rather to complement it, making it not only more understandable, but helping people appreciate both the grand gestures and the small, intimate movements in the worshiping life of a congregation or parish that reveal the presence of God.

Each session for each celebrated day of the church year begins with the following format:

- Background information—a historical and theological summary of the origin of the feast or holy day.
- Educator's note—special instructions to the educator or lay leader who is leading the activity.
- Materials needed—a short list of materials that will be needed for each session.
- Additional ideas—a list of other activities that could be used for a session.
- Assessment of session—questions at the end of each session so that educators and the class can assess the effectiveness of the lesson.
- Further resources—a list of other resources for some of the celebrated days.

In light of the above comment on worship, please note the format of each session. We have purposefully structured it according to a similar format of worship, which is a kind of narrative structure emphasizing a beginning, the middle, and an end to our time together:

- Calling Christ's People Together
- Proclaiming God's Story

- Crafting God's People into God's Story
- Going Out into the World and Living God's Word

We begin this time by calling people together, engaging them in an activity that gathers people to a common task. Next is a reading or presentation of God's story, the Bible, according to the Revised Common Lectionary readings. We then turn our attention to a theme or an idea from God's story according to scripture and how it may be embodied in the gestures performed in and by a Christian community. We close with an activity we can take with us and practice in the place where we Christians live, as Christ commanded us: "Go therefore and make disciples of all nations, baptizing them in the name of the Father and of the Son and of the Holy Spirit, and teaching them to obey everything that I have commanded you" (Matthew 28:19–20).

Each session should take from fifty to sixty minutes to complete, about the same time as a church school class or catechetical session. Because of this time limit, it is our hope that the sessions could be used before worship, possibly around a church breakfast, or after worship, around a potluck lunch. Other people may enjoy using these sessions during a midweek program. However, it is never meant to usurp or replace worship.

The writers of *Sacred Seasons* have created this book with some common assumptions: First, we have presented sessions in which people can either read, write, draw, paint, sing, dance, or move to God's story in the Bible as is their preference or capability. In other words, mindful that not everyone can or will want to read or write, see, or hear the story of the Bible, we have created activities that can be adapted to how one can best communicate with others in our "common" language, expression, or gesture of the Christian faith.

Second, the practices of each session are designed to be "intergenerational." We purposefully created curriculum in which people who are very young, as well as those who are older, may participate in one or more of the activities together at the same time and place. Likewise, these sessions are not to necessarily be done once and then forgotten or crossed off of our "proverbial" checklist. Instead, as those who are Jewish repeat the gestures found in the story of Passover each year, Christians repeat the Christmas story, Epiphany, Shrove Tuesday, Ash Wednesday, Lent, Triduum along with Holy or Passion Week, Ascension Sunday, and Pentecost remembering—in the performance of the gestures assigned to the basic celebration day—our common life in the body of Christ.

Third, these sessions are for all economic or social classes. The materials for the sessions are not expensive and can be found in most any locale or culture. The sessions are also created out of the assumption that people who are either temporarily able-bodied or disabled of mind or body will be participants, though all the activities will need to be adapted with regard to what people can or cannot do in each particular circumstance.

Finally, it is our hope that *Sacred Seasons* may embody Christ's spirit as we teach the congregations and parishes of the God who makes the high holy days and *seasons* we participate in as Christians *sacred* and holy. It is our sincere hope that, with a better understanding of the significance of the days in the church year, we Christians—either Protestant or Catholic—may live more faithfully and in awe of the pilgrimage we have been called to partake in as children of God.

Brett Webb-Mitchell

• ONE •

Advent

Introduction

The word "Advent" means "coming." Christians know and celebrate the season of Advent as a time of preparation and reflection in anticipation of Christmas, the celebration of Christ's birth. Initially, the Advent season varied from three to seven weeks. Later, it became customary to observe the season for four weeks. We look at Advent as the beginning of the church year, which begins on the Sunday nearest to November 30 and contains the four Sundays before Christmas Day. The liturgical color for Advent is blue or violet. Advent is thought of as a time of penitence and preparation for the coming of Jesus Christ.

The Advent Wreath

The origin of the Advent wreath is unknown. Germany and France are possibly the countries where the tradition began. The original wreath was a circle of wire that represented the unending love of God. Evergreens adorning the wreath symbolized the hope of eternal life that God's people share.

The four candles set in the wreath represented the four weeks of Advent. The candles were given names: the Prophecy Candle, the Bethlehem Candle, the Shepherd's Candle, and the Angels' Candle. Candles match the liturgical color of blue, with the exception of the Shepherd's Candle (third Sunday in Advent), which is pink. The lighting of one candle each week marks the growing anticipation for the light of the world enshrouded in darkness—Jesus Christ.

The Jesse Tree

This Advent tree appeared in early form as designs in stained-glass windows and stonework of large cathedrals in medieval Europe. The images portrayed the lineage of Christ from the line of David, with a figure of Jesse at the base or root of the tree. The tree pictures could number as little as four or as many as fifty. In the Hebrew Scriptures, Jesse was the father of David, a great king of Israel. The Jesse Tree became a symbolic representation of the Hebrew stories, leading to the birth of Christ. The Jesse Tree can be used as an Advent calendar, to remind us that God the creator of the world is also God the redeemer and sustainer of the world.

The Jesse Tree is based on Isaiah 11:1–9, where God promises a king from Jesse's family. Symbols or ornaments for the tree are based on Jesse's ancestors and on prophetic statements that foretold the coming of a new king. Christians interpret the king to be Jesus. Each day during Advent, there is a Bible story to read and a corresponding symbol to hang on the Jesse Tree. The last symbol is the manger and star of Bethlehem.

Educator's Notes

Theme of the Day: How do we prepare for the coming of the Christ child? We speak his name; we practice songs and silence. We study the names and stories of his ancestors from the Old Testament. We look and listen for signs of God with us in the past and present.

Practice of the Day: Focus on four names for the Christ child: Jesus, Savior, Lord, Emmanuel. Use these names during this week.

Materials Needed

- Jesse Tree materials to create individual tree banners:

  Burlap or other suitable cloth material, cut 15 by 28 inches for each banner.

  One small dowel rod per banner, 16–18 inches long.

  Fabric glue, masking tape, or small pieces of Velcro to attach tree leaves.

  Green cloth felt or fabric, one square per tree, approx. 8 x 10 inches per square.

  Paper reproductions of the Jesse Tree symbols.
- Jesse Tree symbols and explanation of symbols (to be prepared ahead of time).
- Jesse Tree reproductions on paper, enough for each person to have their own.
- Advent Wreath for the entire group to use in activity.
- Advent Wreath materials to create individual wreaths:

  Round Styrofoam ring, any size.

  Four Advent candles, any size: three blue, one pink.

  Green leaves, evergreen branches, and colored ribbon to decorate wreaths (optional).

- Music: Hymn arrangement of "Oh, Come, Oh Come Emmanuel."
- Tape or compact disc of hymn (or another Christmas or Advent carol) if no accompanist is available.
- Bibles; one per four people.

Practicing the Story

Calling Christ's People Together *(10 minutes)*

Prepare ahead of time Jesse Tree symbols and explanations. Make two sets of individual Jesse Tree symbols to be used in the gathering exercise. Paper reproductions would be sufficient.

1. Gather the people in the fellowship hall or designated meeting area. Each person picks up a Jesse Tree symbol. When all are distributed, have the people find a partner(s) that matches their symbols. Sit down in selected location.
2. Write the following words on chalkboard, wipe-board, overhead projector, or poster board: "Jesus during Advent"; "Savior during Advent"; "Lord during Advent"; "Emmanuel during Advent." As a larger group or in smaller groups, discuss the following:

   How do we prepare to celebrate the coming of Jesus-Savior-Lord-Emmanuel during Advent?

   List answers on the board for all to see. How does our church prepare for Jesus-Savior-Lord-Emmanuel? List any changes in liturgy, special banners, prayers, or music. Write the Bible verse "Be still, and know that I am God!" (Psalm 46:10) on the board.

Practice silence or prayer for one minute.

Proclaiming God's Story *(15 minutes)*

Revised Common Lectionary for Advent Season

Advent 1

Cycle A: Isaiah 2:1–5; Psalm 122; Romans 13:11–14; Matthew 24:36–44

Cycle B: Isaiah 64:1–9; Psalm 80:1–7, 17–19; 1 Corinthians 1:3–9; Mark 13:24–37

Cycle C: Jeremiah 33:14–16; Psalm 25:1–9; 1 Thessalonians 3:9–13; Luke 21:25–36

Advent 2

Cycle A: Isaiah 11:1–10; Psalm 72:1–7, 18–19; Romans 15:4–13; Matthew 3:1–12

Cycle B: Isaiah 40:1–11; Psalm 85:1–2, 8–13; 2 Peter 3:8–15a; Mark 1:1–8

Cycle C: Malachi 3:1–4; Luke 1:68–79; Philippians 1:3–11; Luke 3:1–6

Advent 3

Cycle A: Isaiah 35:1–10; Psalm 146:4–9; James 5:7–10; Matthew 11:2–11

Cycle B: Isaiah 61:1–4, 8–11; Psalm 126; 1 Thessalonians 5:16–24; John 1:6–8, 19–28

Cycle C: Zephaniah 3:14–20; Isaiah 12:2–6; Philippians 4:4–7; Luke 3:7–18

Advent 4

Cycle A: Isaiah 7:10–16; Psalm 80:1–7, 16–18; Romans 1:17; Matthew 1:18–25

Cycle B: 2 Samuel 7:1–11, 16; Luke 1:47–55; Hebrews 10:5–10; Luke 1:39–45

1. Divide into smaller groups, with one Bible per group. Each group is assigned one of the Lesson Focus passages (multiple groups may use the same passage).

   Lesson Focus: Jesus: Acts 22:6–8

   Savior: John 4:39–42

   Lord: John 20:26–29

   Emmanuel: Matthew 1:23

   Challenge: Locate three other scripture passages that use the name referenced as the assigned passage (Jesus, Savior, Lord, Emmanuel).
2. Place an Advent wreath on a table or in a visible place for all to see. Remove the four candles and give them to four participants to hold. Share background of Advent wreath from the introduction.
3. Designate a leader to read the following four sentences to the group. After each sentence is read, the group repeats it as a person holding a candle places it in the Advent wreath.

Leader: We call you Jesus. *(Group repeats as candle is placed in wreath.)*

Leader: We call you Savior.

Leader: We call you Lord.

Leader: We call you Emmanuel.

Crafting God's People into God's Story (*20 minutes*)

1. Name the ancestors and the prophetic symbols of the Jesse Tree ornaments. As each ornament is named, discuss briefly the Hebrew Scripture story associated with the name. As the ornament is discussed, it can be brought forward and hung by a participant on a banner or a standing tree.
2. Make individual Jesse Trees. Families may wish to make a single tree for the home. Cut green fabric felt leaves for the tree and glue the paper print of each symbol on the felt. Using masking tape or small, cut pieces of Velcro, attach the leaves to the tree.
3. If time permits (or in place of the Jesse Tree), make individual Advent wreaths. Have materials and supplies ready. Family groups can create Advent wreaths for the home, Sunday school classrooms, catechesis classroom, for friends, or for anyone!

Going Out into the World and Living God's Word (*10 minutes*)

1. Gather group in a selected area and bring finished Jesse Trees or Advent wreaths, if possible. Create an atmosphere of darkness. Practice one minute of silence as the group prepares for closing prayers. Following silence, explain how darkness filled the world before the birth of Jesus. The people of God long ago waited for a Savior, Lord, Emmanuel: God with us.

We, too, anticipate his coming again into our homes, our lives. Just as we prepare for a guest by cleaning, cooking, and decorating, we can prepare for Jesus-Savior-Lord-Emmanuel by leaving behind our "busyness" and being still. Light an Advent candle each week. Remember the darkness and anticipate Christ's return. Reflect on Christ's family tree—the line of David and his descendants. Christ is our past, present, and future.

Leader:	Let us pray. For you, O Jesus, my soul in stillness waits.
Response:	**Truly my hope is in you.**
Leader:	For you, O Savior, my soul in stillness waits.
Response:	**Truly my hope is in you.**
Leader:	For you, O Lord, my soul in stillness waits.
Response:	**Truly my hope is in you.**
Leader:	For you, Emmanuel, my soul in stillness waits.
Response:	**Truly my hope is in you. Amen.** (Psalm 33:20–22; Psalm 62:1)

Charge to the people: God is coming into our world. Be still and wait for him. The peace of the coming Jesus-Savior-Lord-Emmanuel be present with you always. Greet each other with God's peace:

Leader:	The peace of Christ be with you;
People:	**And also with you.**

Share the peace of Christ, saying "Peace of Christ" when shaking hands or hugging one another.

Additional Ideas

1. The lineage of Christ is found in the Gospel of Matthew 1. Another Bible study related to the Jesse Tree might be to look at the passages in the book of Samuel regarding the anointing of David as king and compare this to other Hebrew Scripture prophecies of future kings.
2. Create an Advent dance to be performed around an Advent wreath.
3. Create prayers for the Advent season.
4. Host a Jesse Tree- or Advent wreath-making workshop during Advent.
5. During the season of Advent, gather for services of quiet meditation, silence, and prayer.

Evaluation Questions to Ponder

1. Do Christians hold different views regarding the God of the Hebrew Scriptures (the God of Jesse and David) and the God of the Christian Scriptures (Jesus)? The Jesse Tree is a way to connect the love of God in the Hebrew Scriptures and the love of God in the Christian Scriptures as seen throughout the lives of God's people. In what ways do we reinforce the fact that the God of the Hebrew and Christian Scriptures is the same God?
2. Total silence is a difficult thing to achieve. Why is it perceived as difficult? How can we be more comfortable with silence? How do our worship practices reflect the need for quiet meditation?

3. Look for ways to reinforce the practices of Advent in the home. Advent wreaths and Jesse Trees are ways; there are many others.

Resources

1. Breckenridge, Marilyn S. *Jesse Tree Devotions: A Family Activity for Advent.* Minneapolis, Minn.: Augsburg Fortress, 1985.
2. Grant, Debra R. *The Jesse Tree: Personal Devotions to Help Christians Grow during Advent.* St. Louis, Mo.: Creative Communications for the Parish, 1992.
3. James, Darcy. *Let's Make a Jesse Tree!* Nashville, Tenn.: Abingdon Press, 1988.
4. Philippart, David, and Laura Montenegro. *Welcome, Yule!* Chicago, Ill.: Liturgy Training Publications, 1996.
5. *Whose Birthday Is It Anyway?* Christmas Alternatives, P.O. Box 1707, Forest Park, Ga. 30502.

• TWO •

Christmas

Introduction

Christmas, or "the mass of Christ," is the day on which we celebrate the birth of Jesus Christ. While the term originated in the eleventh century, it was decided in 354 C.E. that Christmas was to be held on December 25.

Christmastide begins on Christmas Eve and continues until the Sunday after Epiphany. The twelve days of Christmas are counted from Christmas to Epiphany. Twelfth Night marks the end of the Christmas season and often means one last extraordinary party.

The actual day of Christmas has gone through many changes, especially in emphasis. For example, Christmas was a most popular celebration in Europe during the Middle Ages, but during the Reformation, the celebration of Christmas declined, only to be restored in the seventeenth century. In New England, Christmas was outlawed until 1870, and pupils missing school because of Christmas were punished or dismissed. Because of the later influx of Irish Catholics into the New England area, however, there was a return to the Christmas holidays.[1] Now, America as a culture is swept up into the Christian holy day of Christmas.

The liturgical color for Christmas is white.

Educator's Notes

THEME OF THE DAY: The birth of the Christ child, as the fulfillment of the promise made by God to the people of Israel. This is the Messiah, the anointed One, of Jesse's Tree.

PRACTICE OF THE DAY: Giving a gift of time, energy, or talent to the church, the body of Christ, in the coming year—"A Gift from One of the Children of God."

Materials Needed

- A Christmas tree. This could be connected with Advent if the congregation or parish chooses to have a Jesse Tree. The same tree can be used with only the symbols on the tree changing, keeping some of the symbols on, this time making the Jesse Tree a chrismon tree.
- Small sheets of white foam or Styrofoam in which pins can be used, or glue in decorating as chrismon symbols.
- A knife or sharp scissors may need to be used to cut the Styrofoam.
- White construction paper or tag or poster board.
- Scissors.
- Gold, silver, or yellow markers.
- Gold or silver glitter.
- Glue.

- Individual, small, hand-held candles, with paper babushkas around the base, and matches.
- Multicolored construction paper.
- Robes, towels, and other items that may be used for the nativity scene.
- Christmas hymns on tape.
- Wrapping paper and cards for the purpose of "Giving a Gift from One of the Children of God."

Practicing the Story

CALLING CHRIST'S PEOPLE TOGETHER *(10 minutes)*

1. Chrismon Tree: As suggested above and in the previous lesson, Advent is a good time to set up a Jesse Tree on which there are symbols that remind us of God's love and compassion as foretold in the story of Jesse, who was King David's father.

   For the chrismon tree, we can take some of the symbols that reminded us of the promise God made to a discouraged nation of Israel and use them as the fulfillment of that promise in the birth of the Christ child.

   "Chrismon" is a combination of two words: "Christ" and "monogram." The chrismon symbols are made of gold and white, since white is the liturgical color for Christmas and represents the purity and perfection of Christ. The gold represents the majesty and glory of Christ.

   What is proposed is making some chrismons out of Styrofoam or, especially for children, cutting some of the symbols out of white construction paper. Have some models or stencils for the chrismon symbols so that people can trace and cut out the ornaments. When finished, either leave to dry, if need be, or hang on the tree.

As an alternative, some chrismon symbols can be made out of art dough. If so, have the dough ready to be shaped and molded into chrismon symbols. The recipe for art dough is as follows: 2 cups flour, 1 cup salt, and 1 cup water. Knead dough for 7–10 minutes. Bake at 325 degrees for 35–60 minutes, depending on the thickness. Paint and decorate afterwards.

Keep the tree up until Epiphany, January 6.

2. Have some food and drink available as people make their decorations.
3. If possible, have some Christmas music playing in the background.

Proclaiming God's Story *(10 minutes)*

Revised Common Lectionary Reading for Christmas

Christmas Eve:

Isaiah 9:2–7; Psalm 96; Titus 2:11–14; Luke 2:1–14

Nativity of Jesus Christ-Christmas Day (Morning):

Isaiah 62:6–12; Psalm 97; Titus 3:4–7; Luke 2:8–20

Nativity of Jesus Christ-Christmas Day:

Isaiah 52:7–10; Psalm 98; Hebrews 1:1–4; John 1:1–14

Crafting God's People into God's Story *(20–25 minutes)*

1. The Un-rehearsed Christmas Play

While many churches perform Christmas plays and spectacles during Advent, we propose that the re-creation of the nativity scene be done on either Christmas Eve or Christmas Day, following Luke 2:1–20 as the "script."

What is suggested by the term "un-rehearsed" is the hope to get as many people as humanly possible involved in the telling of the Christmas story. Each person could have a part, from playing one among the many angels, shepherds, or cattle and sheep, to being "primary actors," like Mary, Joseph, and the narrator.

Have some bathrobes or other loose-fitting clothes for people to wear as robes and towels for headdresses. Cut out paper ears and tails for sheep and donkeys.

Wings for angels can be made from cardboard or fabric and wire. Some hay or dry grass can be used to suggest a stable, with the appropriate animal noises when necessary.

The "actors" should be given minimal direction and placed in an area known as "the stage." While the narrator reads the story, people simply assume their places in this "living tableau" of the nativity scene. Music or rhythm instruments may also be used to announce the different players in this story.

It would be appropriate to begin this time singing something like "Away in a Manger" or "Silent Night" and end with something like "Hark the Herald Angels Sing" or "O Come, All Ye Faithful."

2. A "Gift from One of the Children of God"

Having watched, heard, seen, or been a participant in the "Un-Rehearsed Christmas Play," sing a hymn or two and focus on the gift God has given to the world this day—his only begotten son. Read John 3:16.

In response to this gift from God, pass out a piece of paper or a card to each person. Have them think of one gift that they might give to the life of the church this coming year. It should be a gift of time, energy, and talent, for the building up of the body of Christ. It could be time working in the nursery or baby-sitting, cleaning out a closet in a church, raking someone's lawn, shoveling a snow-clogged driveway, cutting someone's lawn, cooking dinner for the soup kitchen, or driving the youth group to a mission project. For those who may not choose something to do, they may give money so that others may participate.

After people have had time to think about their gift, have them write it on the paper or card and put the gift under the chrismon tree, to perhaps be opened on Epiphany at another gathering of the people of God.

Going Out into the World and Living God's Word *(10 minutes)*

1. Caroling: This may be the most appropriate time and season to go singing and visiting people who are shut in and unable, for one reason or another, to attend church for this occasion. But, maybe, instead of visiting those who are unable to attend church on Christmas Day, a good time to visit may be a week or two *after*

Christmas Day. Discuss sending "teams" of six or seven people out to visit others, and discuss where they should go. Prepare a list of people to be visited beforehand and have maps and instructions about the people ready to be handed out. Next, pray for those who are visiting and to be visited.

2. End this time with one another with this sentence of scripture and prayer:

Leader: The Word became flesh and dwelt among us, full of grace and truth.

People: We have beheld his glory. Alleluia!

Leader: O God, we are swept up in the wonder
of this beautiful mystery.
With shepherds and magi, Mary and Joseph,
We come to adore the Christ-child.
With our lives, we present our gifts of faith,
hope, and love to the Savior.
Amen.

Sing "Joy to the World!"

Additional Ideas

1. There are many books and encyclopedias with information on the origin of many of the traditions we practice during Christmas. Discuss the reason we have Christmas trees, the purpose of having lights on the tree, Yule logs, lights around the house or in the windows, as well as the origin of Santa Claus and St. Nicholas.

2. Name and discuss how Christians in other countries celebrate this holy day of Christmas. Perhaps have booths or learning centers, as in a carnival or market, of Christmas celebrations from other lands and among other Christians.

Evaluation Questions to Ponder

1. Did people make the connection between the symbol of the chrismon tree and the Christmas story?
2. Did it work to tie in the chrismon tree and the Jesse tree?
3. What kinds of gifts did people give to the church? How could we broaden the gifts given to the congregation or parish to include other congregations and parishes who are in more need of assistance or whose needs are different from the congregation that practiced this activity?

• THREE •

Epiphany

Introduction

Epiphania, the Greek root word for "Epiphany," means manifestation or revelation. On Epiphany, we have revealed to us the other side of the mystery of the incarnation: "This tiny, helpless child in the straw is also the God and ruler of our universe. All of our Advent prayers of longing for a Lord and Savior have come true."[1] With Epiphany, we also contemplate the mysteries of Jesus' infancy. The presentation of Jesus at the Temple, the flight into Egypt, Mary's visitation to Elizabeth, and the song of Zechariah all reveal the mystery of the long-awaited Messiah who we see at the same time is sought and adored and rejected. The light will make manifest the darkness. We enter the season of Epiphany with the Lord of all light who shows us that darkness, though not abolished, is made known and overcome. With, in, and through him, by the power of the Holy Spirit, we may see the darkness and not be afraid.

The Epiphany of the Lord is January 6. The liturgical color for the day is white, and the season of Epiphany, which lasts approximately 4–9 weeks, uses the liturgical color green. Epiphany is a celebration of Christ being made known to the Gentiles. The story of the wise men, who came to worship the Christ child, is also part of this season. Jesus is the gift of salvation for all nations. Sharing the good news of Jesus with all people is an important focus during Epiphany. A central theme during Epiphany is God's light overcoming the darkness of sin and evil. Symbols of light, stars (star of Bethlehem), crowns, and gifts (wise men) are used during this time of the church year. The season is flexible in length due to the changing date of Easter each calendar year.

Educator's Notes

THEME OF THE DAY: Jesus is the good news for all nations. We remember the wise men who went to great lengths to meet the Lord. We look to the light of Christ that is reflected in our lives.

PRACTICE OF THE DAY: "Adopting" a country of the world to study during the new year. Writing a letter or having a pen pal. Celebrating Jesus revealed to the world with the eating of Epiphany cake and singing of Epiphany songs. Practicing giving gifts of "light" to others.

Epiphany celebrations come with many varying traditions. In some churches, it is customary to hold a burning of the greens on the eve of Epiphany, January 5. Eating Epiphany cake is another tradition. In some parts of Europe, an Epiphany king or queen is crowned. Later in the church year, the king or queen serves as the "host" of the Shrove Tuesday Carnival the evening before Ash Wednesday.

The following suggested activities reflect the worship of a community of Christians, as well as the charge from God to go into the world and minister as "lights of Christ." Connecting foreign countries and places in the world far and near with the revelation of Jesus in the world is important. It is a manifestation of Christian awareness that we are part of a global world, a larger creation. We are called to be brothers and sisters to all people, especially those we have not met.

Materials Needed

- A recipe for Epiphany cake: Any white cake recipe will do, the richer the better. Include white icing. Make an Epiphany cake prior to the celebration, large enough for everyone to have a small piece. Decorations might include statues of the three wise men, silver or gold stars on the cake, or a crown ornament.
- Candles of all shapes and sizes to be placed on a table and lit during the celebration. Safety considerations should be taken when lighting candles indoors. The number of candles is determined by the leadership (there is no recommendation).
- Song sheets or hymnbooks containing Christmas hymns. Hymn suggestions:

  "I Want to Walk as a Child of the Light." Text: Kathleen Thomerson. Tune: "Houston."

  "What Star Is This." Text: Charles Coffin. Tune: "Puer Nobis."

  "We Three Kings of Orient Are." Text: John Henry Hopkins Jr. Tune: "Three Kings of Orient."

  "We Are Marching in the Light of God." Text: South African. Tune: "Siyahamba."

- Small flags of many nations. Geography stores carry small replicas of national flags. If no real flags are available, look in advance for posters, stickers, or other reproductions of flags of many nations. Plan for enough flags so that every person can take one home. An adjustment to this idea is to give flags only to the children, if cost is an issue.
- Optional: Costumes for three wise men to wear. Bathrobes, belts, crowns made of paper or shiny material, and jewels to be worn around neck. Use fabric or fancy trimmings found in fabric stores to make the costumes interesting.
- Light catchers: Plastic, stained-glass light catchers with various designs may be found in any craft store. Light catchers are hung in windows and reflect the sunlight. Purchase ones to be made by the group, or have premade light catchers available for the celebration. Tissue paper glued to a construction paper frame makes a good homemade light catcher.
- Materials needed for paper light catchers: glue, tissue paper in various colors, and construction paper in any colors, scissors. Check craft store for materials if making plastic light catchers purchased from stores.

Practicing the Story

Calling Christ's People Together *(10 minutes)*

1. Begin by singing hymns and lighting candles on a table in the gathering room. Have song sheets or hymnals available. Begin singing favorite Christmas carols.

   If no music accompanist or instrument is available, sing *a cappella.* Taped music prepared in advance is also acceptable. During the singing, light all of the candles on the table. Candles may also be placed in windows or other parts of the gathering room as is appropriate and safe.

2. Begin with prayer.

   To you, O God, light of lights, we give you thanks. You illumine the beauty of creation in the life of the Christ-child. With your light, we see anew your image in the life of those we meet in our daily lives. To you be all honor and praise. Amen.

Proclaiming God's Story *(10 minutes)*

Revised Common Lectionary Reading for the Epiphany of Our Lord

Cycles A, B, and C: Isaiah 60:1–6; Psalm 72:1–7, 10–14; Ephesians 3:1–12; Matthew 2:1–12

Lesson Focus: Matthew 2:1–12

Crafting God's People into God's Story *(10 minutes)*

1. If desired, select in advance three people to portray the three wise men. It is possible that instead of males, females may assume the roles. There is no proof that there were only three kings; many countries celebrate as many as seventy or more "wise men" coming to see baby Jesus. Three people dressed as wise men may enter the gathering, carrying gifts in their hands: frankincense, gold, and myrrh. (Prepared in advance, any size or shape of box or bottle will work as the "gifts.") Placing their gifts near the candle table, each wise person shares in the reading of the story of the Magi,

Matthew 2:1–12. Following the reading, sing the hymn "We Three Kings of Orient Are."

2. Have participants share in a large or small group the following thoughts:

- Name a place or object of light (examples: flashlight, sun, moon, stars, headlights, lightning).
- Name a place or object of darkness (examples: night, dark clouds, the color black).
- Name a beloved gift received during the Christmas season.

After sharing in large or small groups, spend a few moments in quiet meditation as a hymn is being played (any hymn will work), thinking of the gift of Jesus in the world and in our lives.

3. Discuss the meaning of Epiphany and the season (see the Introduction and Educator's Notes). To think of Jesus as part of the world, we need to think of the world as larger than our church or our own backyard. Name a place in the world far away from your home. Following this exercise, recite: For every candle burning, there is a matching candle in a place on the other side of the world. We are brothers and sisters, connected by Jesus to all people in all places.

   Distribute the nations' flags, one to every person (or family). If there are wise men, they may distribute the flags. Note: Each flag should be marked with the name of the country. Give directions to the people: "Receive a flag of the nations of God's world in remembrance of Jesus' coming to save the world. Spend time this Epiphany learning about your flag and the people of that country. Pray for the people of your 'adopted' nation every day. Consider ways of sharing with others what you have learned."

Break into small groups to create light catchers. Have materials ready on a craft table or craft area. Spend time creating a light catcher for someone you know. Light catchers can be made as gifts for a local nursing home, a local preschool, or a soup kitchen. The light catcher is another reminder of the light of Christ made present in the incarnation.

Going Out into the World and Living God's Word *(10 minutes)*

1. Revisit the story of the wise men. What do you think the wise men said when first catching a glimpse of the baby Jesus after their long journey to find the King? Have the group create a sentence of greeting to Jesus that everyone can say together. (For example, "Welcome, Lord Jesus!" "Hail to the King!" "Glory be to God!"). Practice this greeting together several times.
2. End with a prayer.

   You call us together, as your body, O Christ, to be bearers of peace. As the Prince of Peace, teach us to bring your peace to a world on the edge of divisions. Unite us in your love, we pray. Amen.
3. Share in the feasting on Epiphany cake and fellowship.

Additional Ideas

1. Assign different families or church groups particular responsibilities for the Epiphany celebration: Candle

set up, cake-making, craft-making, wise men costumes. Involve as many different people as possible in the preparation for this event.

2. Burn incense as part of the celebration. Discuss the uses for frankincense, gold, and myrrh. (Check the encyclopedia for information.) Be mindful when using incense: Some people present may be allergic to strong smells.
3. If burning of the greens is practiced, and a safe place is possible to do this, the Christmas tree may be burned as Christmas carols are sung. Perhaps participants could bring their trees from home to make a larger bonfire. Check local fire permits before undertaking such activities.
4. Invite neighboring churches to the Epiphany activities.
5. Provide opportunity for follow-up sharing about the flags of the nations. Provide a time for everyone to share what they have learned about each country. Begin a mission project that might benefit one or more countries.

Evaluation Questions to Ponder

1. How do we keep the "Christmas season" in our hearts all year? How do Epiphany activities help keep the theme of Christmas-tide alive?
2. Discuss the brightness of one candle vs. the brightness of many candles. Are we called to be lights of Christ alone or with others? How can we discover ways to be a community of "candles"?
3. Could you leave your "kingdom" or "dominion" and travel in search of a new king as the wise men did? Why or why not? What hardships do you think the wise men endured? What do you imagine happened to them after they saw Jesus? Create a story.

• FOUR •

The Baptism of Jesus

Introduction

The baptism of Jesus falls on the first Sunday after Epiphany. The liturgical color of the day is white. The liturgical calendar can be seen as a means of catechism, teaching and equipping the saints for ministry. The celebration of "holy days" will help the body of Christ grow together in the understanding and practice of our faith.

The baptism of Jesus is a grand occasion for celebrating our baptism and its meaning in our Christian life. The lessons for the day reflect the event of Jesus' baptism and the beginning of his ministry life as recorded in the Gospels. The four Gospel stories of the baptism of Jesus contain different details of the event. What is important to remember is that God pours out his unconditional love and Holy Spirit on Jesus and, thus, equips him for ministry in the world.

Educator's Notes

THEME OF THE DAY: The water imagery in baptism. God's loving words: "You are my beloved, in whom I am well pleased." Through water and the Word we are made children of God.

PRACTICE OF THE DAY: Create through artwork (drawing, painting, or sculpting) a renewed picture of water and Word, Baptism. Take home!

It is suggested to divide larger groups of fifty or more people into smaller groups. The activities center on a "Journey on the River Jordan" and may require several rooms to create the atmosphere described. Prior to the "journey" portion of the event, a discussion of baptism theology for your denomination would be helpful.

Why do we celebrate Jesus' baptism? The answer to this very important question will hopefully evolve as people travel down the River Jordan.

Have small groups share stories of their own baptisms or a particularly memorable baptism, funny baptism, and so on. How many know the date of their baptism? place? age?

A discussion of water and its uses may also be a helpful preparation for the group. Remember that the River Jordan is water, a common element and an essential one for survival. Stories of water and birth will be shared in our journey. In remembering Jesus' baptism, we remember the ways in which water tells our collective story as the people of God.

Materials Needed

- Blue paper or tarps on the floor to make the River Jordan, connecting the stations.
- Cardboard refrigerator boxes. Cut out two sides of each box opposite each other in order to make the boxes look somewhat like arks. Do not worry about writing on the boxes as they will be decorated with murals and drawings made on paper that can be taped to the sides of the "arks."

- Crayons, markers, paints and brushes at each station.
- Strips of white material from old bedsheets for sashes, approx. 6 inches wide and 3 feet long.
- Tape for the refrigerator boxes.
- Hymnals and Bibles at each station for the leaders to read the liturgy or scripture.
- Hymnals to sing "This Is the Spirit's Entry Now" (or another appropriate hymn from your hymnbook). Alternate tune: "Azmon."

Practicing the Story

Calling Christ's People Together *(10 minutes)*

1. Have the group assemble in the fellowship hall or another suitable meeting place and be seated in chairs set up in the middle of the room. An appropriate opening prayer may be given:

   Oh God, you are the font of every blessing, the Spirit of eternal waters, and the source of all life. Refresh in us, Christ, the meaning of our baptism with the joyful celebration of your baptism in the Jordan. Amen.

2. Sing the hymn "This Is the Spirit's Entry Now" or another appropriate hymn. As groups move between stations, play or sing this hymn that will act as a timekeeper, signaling when it is time for the participants to move ahead.
3. Divide into small groups (10–15 people) and give each group an "ark" made from refrigerator boxes. Stay together in the large room for the reading of scripture.

Proclaiming God's Story

<u>Revised Common Lectionary Reading for the Baptism of Jesus</u>

Cycle A: Isaiah 42:1–9, Psalm 29; Acts 10:34–43; Matthew 3:13–17

Cycle B: Genesis 1:1–5; Psalm 29; Acts 19:1–7; Mark 1:4–11

Cycle C: Isaiah 43:1–7; Psalm 29; Acts 8:14–17; Luke 3:15–17, 21–22

Lesson Focus: Gospel stories in Matthew, Mark, Luke, and in John 1:29–34.

1. Read the Gospel accounts of Jesus' baptism with the entire group assembled.
2. Disperse by small groups, follow the blue path (the River Jordan), and "get aboard" the arks. According to the size of your group, you may wish to disperse each group to one of the three stations, staggering the groups if there are more than three, or sending two at a time to each station. Although this means that the sequential order of the scriptures will not be followed for all groups, the water imagery of the scriptures will be given by traveling to each station.

Crafting God's People into God's Story *(20 minutes)*

1. The Birth and Power of Creation

A member of the small group or a person assigned as leader of this station will read the first third of the "Thanksgiving over the Water" from the Baptismal

Covenant 1 of the *United Methodist Hymnal* or use a similar reading from your book of worship on baptism:

> When nothing existed but chaos, you swept across the dark waters and brought forth light. In the days of Noah you saved those on the ark through water. After the flood you set in the clouds a rainbow. When you saw your people as slaves in Egypt, you led them to freedom through the sea. Their children you brought through the Jordan to the land which you promised.

As an alternative to the above passage, the following may be read: Genesis 1:1–5; 7:1–11, 17–24; 8:1–5, 15–22; 9:12–17; and Exodus 14:21–29. Have large poster paper, crayons, markers, and paint available for the group to draw a mural of the different images they heard in the words spoken. Ask them where (or in what event in the life of the church) they have heard these words spoken. If the liturgy is used, the leader may want to ask which stories they heard in the liturgy in order to get creativity going. When the melody from the hymn is sung or played, it is time to move to the next station.

2. New Birth—By Water and the Spirit

Another member of the small group or leader of the station will read the second third of the liturgy from the *United Methodist Hymnal* (or the liturgy from your denomination):

> In the fullness of time you sent Jesus, nurtured in the water of a womb. He was baptized by John and anointed by your Spirit. He called disciples to share in the baptism of his death and resurrection and to make disciples of all nations.

Alternate text: Any of the Gospel accounts. Add John 3:1–5.

What is Jesus talking about or describing? What does it mean to be born of water and the Spirit? What is your image of the Holy Spirit in your life? Have the group draw pictures or murals or use modeling clay to express the Spirit present at Jesus' baptism, their own baptism, or someone else's baptism. Additional scripture reading: 1 Corinthians 12:13 (optional). When hymn melody is heard, move on.

3. New Birth—New Clothes

Read the final part of the liturgy from the *United Methodist Hymnal* (or the liturgy from your denomination):

> Pour out your Holy Spirit, to bless this gift of water and those who receive it, to wash away their sin and clothe them in righteousness throughout their lives, that dying and being raised with Christ, they may share in his final victory.

Alternate scripture: Galatians 3:27 and Revelation 7:9–14.

Historically, the newly baptized Christians were given white robes as a sign of their spiritual cleansing and righteousness—signifying a new relationship with God through faith in Jesus Christ, who was baptized while he was here on earth. Ask the group to take white strips of material (cut from old bed sheets) and decorate them with baptismal signs, imagery, and words, with the idea that these sashes will be given to people as they are baptized throughout the year. People may want to work individually or collectively on the sashes and may take them home to work on them. At the playing of the hymn tune, all groups should return to the large gathering room and sit in chairs. Remain nearby or with your smaller group.

4. Decorating the Ark: Have each group take their mural drawings and attach them to all sides of their ark. Place the arks on display in the narthex or other appropriate area.

Going Out into the World and Living God's Word *(10 minutes)*

1. All participants close the event by singing the last verse of "This Is the Spirit's Entry Now" or another appropriate hymn.
2. If possible, this would be an appropriate time to incorporate a reaffirmation of baptismal vows for the gathered group. Use the appropriate text from your book of worship.
3. Charge the group with the task of finding the date of their baptisms. Place a book or bulletin board in the church for people to record their dates.

Additional Ideas

1. Invite the parents of the newly baptized (past six months) to be introduced at some point in the gathering. Form a support group for the newly baptized, including those who will be baptized as well as family and friends. Offer support, love, and continuing nurture of the "church's child."
2. Create a "baptismal backpack." What are the gifts of our baptism that can be placed in our backpacks for our journey? Add this preparation for the group as part of preparation to travel the River Jordan.
3. Show a slide presentation or movie documentary on the River Jordan.

Evaluation Questions to Ponder

1. How can we support one another in living our baptisms? What does it mean, to "live our baptism"?
2. Be aware during the preparation for this event that all participants may not be baptized or have any theological references to why baptism is important. The whole community requires careful welcoming of these pilgrims. How can we embrace those who are not baptized?
3. Where is the baptismal font in your church? What does the location of the font say about the importance of Baptism in the parish? How can the font be made visible on a daily basis?

• FIVE •

The Transfiguration

Introduction

Transfiguration Sunday is the last Sunday after Epiphany and is followed by the first Sunday in Lent. The scripture accounts found in Matthew 17:1–9, Mark 9:2–10, and Luke 9:28–36 tell the story of how Jesus took Peter, James, and John to the top of a mountain. On the mountain Jesus was transformed or transfigured before them. From a cloud, a voice said: "This is my Son, the Beloved, with him I am well pleased; listen to him" (Matthew 17:5, NRSV).

The Transfiguration story, like the story of Jesus' baptism, defines Jesus as God's son who will follow his father's will and follow the way to the cross. The event shows us the glory of God: "his face shone like the sun, and his clothes became dazzling white" (Matthew 17:2). It shows us worship: "let us make three dwellings, one for you, one for Moses, one for Elijah" (Luke 9:33).

In each Transfiguration account, the disciples were filled with fear. Matthew 17:7 reads: "But Jesus came and touched them, saying, 'Get up and do not be afraid.'" In this frightful moment, Jesus cares for them and shows them the way. Matthew adds the direction "listen to him." Jesus calls his friends to be followers and listeners. He wants them to not be frightened, but to be courageous.

The word "transfigure" comes from the Latin word *transfigurare* which means to shape, fashion, figure. *Webster's Dictionary* gives the definition: "To give new and typically exalted or spiritual appearance to; to transform outwardly and usually for the better."[1]

The liturgical color of the day is white.

Educator's Notes

THEME OF THE DAY: Jesus is the way of transfiguration. He is our light and our guide. God tells us to listen to him. He left the mountain to live in the valley where a tree in the form of a cross was planted. Jesus has gone before us and will accompany us along the journey of Christian life.

PRACTICE OF THE DAY: Use the greeting, "The Lord be with you," and the response, "And also with you." Learn the task of the acolyte in worship.

Materials Needed

- Drawing paper and drawing supplies, markers, pens, and pencils.
- Display area to share pictures, display the word "Transfiguration."
- Simple costumes for skit: white bed linen, albs, choir robes (optional).
- Flashlights, one or several depending upon the size of group.
- Altar candles or large candle tapers in holders.

- Paper cups to collect snow or hold ice and water.
- Tape or CD player, tapes or CDs of hymns, if no accompanist is available.
- Hymn suggestions: "Silent Night, Holy Night" or "This Little Light of Mine."

Practicing the Story

Calling Christ's People Together *(10 minutes)*

1. Gather the people in song and prayer. Peter said to Jesus, "Lord, it is good for us to be here" (Matthew 17:4). Begin with the singing of songs. Hymn suggestions (use other appropriate hymns from your tradition):

   "How Good Lord to be Here." Text: J. Robinson. Tune: "Potsdam."

   "I Want to Walk as a Child of the Light." Text and Tune: Kathleen Thomerson.

   "Christ, Whose Glory Fills the Skies." Text: Charles Wesley. Tune: "Ratisbon."

   Open with prayer.

   Leader: The Lord be with you.

   Response: And also with you.

   Leader: Let us pray.

   Like Moses and Elijah, we are in awe of the mystery of faith revealed to us on this Transfiguration Day. Take our lives, Lord, this day, and may we be transfigured within you. Amen.

2. Cloud Watching. If weather permits, find a place outside and watch the cloud formations. Let imagina-

tions soar and take turns pointing out different pictures in the clouds. Can anyone see God in the clouds?

3. Supply construction paper and drawing supplies. Ask people to draw a picture or symbol of God. Pictures will be different—there is no right or wrong. No one knows what God looks like—it is a mystery. Display the finished pictures. The sharing of drawings may occur immediately or at the end of the gathering as the leadership chooses.

Proclaiming God's Story *(10 minutes)*

Revised Common Lectionary Reading for the Transfiguration

Cycle A: Exodus 24:12–18; Psalm 2; 2 Peter 1:16–21; Matthew 17:1–9

Cycle B: 2 Kings 2:1–12; Psalm 50:1–6; 2 Corinthians 4:3–6; Mark 9:2–9

Cycle C: Exodus 34:29–35; Psalm 99; 2 Corinthians 3:12—4:2; Luke 9:28–36

Lesson focus for activities: Matthew 17:1–9.

Crafting God's People into God's Story *(20–25 minutes)*

1. Display the word "transfiguration" and help the group define it. Encourage the group to memorize the word and its meaning. Have participants act out the transfiguration story as a narrator reads the Matthew text. Divide a large group into smaller groups if desired. Flashlights and simple costumes, such as white bed

linen, might be used to "light up" the three figures of Moses, Elijah, and Jesus.

2. God adopts us at our baptism and calls us to live in Christ's transfiguration as forgiven children. We can become aware of God working in our lives through everyday, ordinary transformations. Experiment: When possible, gather snow in one small cup, and fill another cup with water. Both are the same substance, only one has been changed and transformed! Use pictures of snow if the real thing is not available or create a pile of ice shavings. An ice cube can also be used in place of snow.

3. God calls us to be followers and listeners. Play a listening game such as the one suggested below.

   Experiment: How do we prepare for worship? Gather the group in a circle(s). Sometimes we sit quietly and listen. Another way we prepare is to greet one another with special words: "The Lord be with you," and the response, "And also with you." Begin to pass the greeting around the circle by whispering it softly. When the greeting completes the circle, say it loud: "The Lord be with you." "And also with you." Listen for the greeting during future worship times and events.

4. On the mountain, Jesus' face shone bright like the sun. We are called to be his light in the world. Light can transform. If possible, light a tall Paschal candle (or a large candle in a holder) in the center of the room. Turn off all lights and notice the light shapes seen in the darkness. Pass a flashlight(s) around the group and

notice how the light changes the face of the person holding the light. Extinguish the Paschal candle and imagine the flame continuing to burn inside each person. Christ shines in us.

5. Serving as acolytes in worship. The person who lights the candles for worship is called an acolyte. The word "acolyte" comes from a Latin word that means "follower." The acolyte assists the body of Christ in worship by caring for the light of Christ. Acolytes usually wear albs and may or may not process and recess with the crucifer during worship. Acolytes have been used in churches as far back as 1,700 years ago. Share with the participants the tasks of acolytes in the parish. Demonstrate proper candle lighting and extinguishing using an acolyte pole and altar candles if appropriate. Discuss what kind of "transformation" takes place when an acolyte wears an alb and performs his or her tasks. This may be an opportunity to enlist a few newcomers to serve as acolytes for future worship.

Going Out into the World and Living God's Word *(10 minutes)*

1. Close with the following readings: Psalm 50:1–6; Psalm 99:1–5.
2. Sing a hymn(s) as closing. "Silent Night" or "This Little Light of Mine."
3. Return to the images of God drawn in the opening exercise. The Transfiguration shows a divine image of God in Jesus in the splendor and the glory on the

mountain. We also see a human image of God in Jesus who will reach out to us when we fall to the ground. These are the images of a loving God, walking with us as we come down from the mountain. Let us go forth as listeners, followers, and disciples.

Go in peace, serve the Lord, do not be afraid for God is with you. Amen.

Additional Ideas

Include a few stories about clouds and the sky. Some suggestions are: Peter Spier, *Dreams* (New York: Trumpet Club, 1991) and Charles G. Shaw, *It Looked Like Spilt Milk* (New York: HarperCollins, 1992).

Other resources containing Transfiguration ideas:

Dennis C. Benson, *Dennis Benson's Creative Bible Studies* (Loveland, Colo.: Group Books, 1991)

Sonja M. Stewart and Jerome W. Berryman, *Young Children and Worship* (Louisville, Ky.: Westminster/John Knox Publishers, 1989)

Evaluation Questions to Ponder

1. Was it difficult to imagine what God looks like? Why or why not?
2. If we are transformed through Jesus Christ, how will we keep the flame burning?
3. What are some common practices we can do together as Christians?
4. Find the places in worship where the greeting "The Lord be with you" is used.

• SIX •

Lent

Shrove Tuesday and Ash Wednesday

Introduction

Lent is a time of penance in which we remember not only our sins but also Jesus Christ's sacrifice for us and our salvation so that we can live anew at Easter with Christ's resurrection. When Pope St. Gregory decreed that Lent should have no meat, the Sunday before Lent became known as Carnevala (farewell to meat), from which came the word "carnival." The carnival became a time to clean out the meat and fats from the cupboard so that fasting could begin on Ash Wednesday, the beginning of Lent. In the early Christian church, people often went to confession the day before Ash Wednesday. This day of confession became known as Shrove Tuesday, because the confessed were forgiven (shriven) of their sins.[1]

How do we prepare for the dying of Christ? The church prepares with the opposite of dying. Shrove Tuesday is about opposites: Instead of fasting, we feast. We play out our inner opposites by coming to the feast in costume. Through the fun of dressing up, "the rich are made poor, authority is dethroned, and fools rule."[2] Shrove Tuesday is a time to poke fun of ourselves and our rules, lest we take them too seriously. In doing so, we return to a brief moment of chaos. Shrove Tuesday makes space for our negative, irrational, and steamy sides. It can be a creative outlet for our inner tensions. It allows us to be with our vulnerable and sinful parts of ourselves.

It has been said that a "Carnival is the ritual hint at what lies behind our desire for the Holy."[3] Through the play of Shrove Tuesday, rituals give us space to identify our darkest struggles and gain insight into our desire to know God. It prepares us to come to the place of confession, and then to receive forgiveness as part of Ash Wednesday. There is no liturgy or liturgical color for Shrove Tuesday (although it can be a very colorful celebration).

Shrove Tuesday can be a time to eat all the sweet and savory foods left in the pantry. One way to use up eggs, milk, and fats was to add flour and make special pancakes. In England, Shrove Tuesday is called Pancake Day, and the festivities include the eating of pancakes. In other parts of the world, there are parades (often called Mardi Gras) and parties of all kinds. Shrove Tuesday is also known as Fat Tuesday.

The activity plan for a carnival is designed for anytime during the week before Ash Wednesday and Lent. The church has celebrated carnival on Shrove Tuesday, but a weekend night is acceptable. The celebration is different in that it does not center itself on one biblical story, but prepares us to engage in Lent, Passion Week, Easter, and Pentecost.

Educator's Notes

THEME OF THE DAY: A celebration of merrymaking, in preparation for Lent.

PRACTICE OF THE DAY: Dancing, playing games, party chaos, ending in devotions. Invite the whole church to the carnival. Include in the invitation a short explanation of Lent and how we prepare for it with the carnival. Invite the congregation to come in costumes portraying the opposite part of them. Also invite them to bring their favorite desserts.

Materials Needed

- Invitations, stamps (sent in advance).
- Extra clothes for costumes and clown makeup.
- Pencils and paper for each participant.
- Small container in which to safely burn paper.
- Matches.
- Kazoos.
- Variety of party music and appropriate tape or CD player.
- Party games: checkers, chess, card decks.
- Card tables or other tables and chairs, set up in advance.
- Prayer of confession.

Practicing the Story

CALLING CHRIST'S PEOPLE TOGETHER *(10 minutes)*

Welcome guests and thank them for coming to the party. Encourage people to mingle and act out their costume characters. Have a table of extra dress-up clothes and make up for people to use if they came without a costume.

Proclaiming God's Story (see Ash Wednesday) *(10 minutes)*

Crafting God's People into God's Story *(20 minutes)*

1. Start with some structured party activities as listed below, and then give people some free time. The following list contains suggestions for party ideas. Consult any party book or similar resource for other options:
   - Circle Dance: Have people join hands and form a circle. Instruct people to step two steps to the right and two steps to the left. Add funny arm movements to the beat of the music. Individuals may introduce a new motion or step as the dance continues.
   - Parade: Line up and hold hands. Give everyone kazoos. Parade through the church and neighborhood. Wheelchairs and strollers are welcome.
   - Silly Chaos: Come back into the church and indulge in favorite desserts, play music, tell jokes, dance, mingle, relax.
2. For those who are less mobile, have a supply of board games, such as checkers, or card decks available for people to play. Card tables may be helpful to encourage small group play.
3. Hold a scavenger hunt in or outside of the church. Make a list of church items to find or mark on a sheet of paper.

Going Out into the World and Living God's Word *(10 minutes)*

1. Sing "Alleluia, Praise Ye the Lord" or a similar song in rounds. This can be sung as a stand up-sit down motion song.

2. Pass out paper and pencils. Give people time to draw or write their confessions of sin, whatever distorts their relationship with God. After completion of the task, collect the paper. Pray together a prayer of confession from a denominational hymnbook. Using the small container and matches, burn the confessions, turning them to ashes.
3. Leader closes with dismissal:

    May the god who delights in our worship of him and celebrates with us in our rejoicing of the goodness of God, fill us all with happiness in the life we live with one another.

    The ashes may be saved and added to the ashes for Ash Wednesday.
4. The people clean up and leave in silence.

Additional Ideas

1. Shrove Tuesday is an excellent time to do mask making. Have craft supplies on a table and create a mask using feathers, glitter, and other materials. Wear the mask around the church.
2. Fill out "time cards" for Lent at the end of Shrove Tuesday activities. Answer this question on a card: "What time will you give towards God this Lent?" Sign your name, leave your card in an offering plate, or give to the pastor.

Evaluation Questions to Ponder

Shrove Tuesday goes together with Ash Wednesday. Does the celebration end with the understanding of the Lenten disciplines to come? What does the church offer in terms of observing the Lenten season?

Ash Wednesday

Introduction

In 1099, Pope Urban II decreed that the first day of Lent would be called Ash Wednesday. Lent has at least two possible origins. It was the final intensive period of preparation for catechumens who were under training to be baptized at the Easter Vigil. It was also a post-Epiphany fast of forty days in Egypt, associated with Christ's forty days in the wilderness, which immediately follows the accounting of his baptism in the Synoptic Gospels. In 325 C.E., the Council of Nicea first referred to Lent as "forty days" and that it comes immediately before Easter. The forty days do not include Sundays because even during Lent, Sundays are always "little Easters." Since Sundays are not part of Lent, it is crucial to have midweek services during Lent so that the congregation can observe Lent together.[4]

Lent is a time of penance. Lent is a time of self-examination, repentance, and turning toward God. The church has historically observed Lent through the disciplines of prayer, fasting, and almsgiving. Through this season we open ourselves to examine our abilities as well as the limitations of our lives. We remember that "you are dust, and to dust you will return" (Genesis 2:7). In our dying, we are preparing to be raised up with Jesus on Easter morning.

After engaging in the good chaos of carnival, the order of worship for the service of Ash Wednesday found in your denomination's book of worship is the way Ash Wednesday can be observed. Remember to use the ashes from the sins burned at the carnival or on Shrove Tuesday during the imposition of ashes. It is also customary in some denominations to use the ashes from the burned palm branches from last year's Palm Sunday celebration.

In contrast to the color and celebration of the carnival, the visual environment should be solemn and stark. Purple or violet is the liturgical color for Lent; for Ash Wednesday, the liturgical color is black and, in some traditions, violet. Rough, coarse textures and dark earth colors suggest the character of the day and season.

Educator's Notes

THEME STORY OF THE DAY: You are dust, and to dust you will return. Confession and forgiveness, prayer and offering of self.

PRACTICE OF THE DAY: The imposition of ashes on foreheads, being marked with the sign of the cross. The worship liturgy is taken from the *United Methodist Book of Worship.* Other denominations will have similar liturgies. Eucharist can also be celebrated on Ash Wednesday.

Materials Needed

- *Book of Worship* from your denomination, containing hymns and liturgy.
- Ashes.
- Bibles.

Practicing the Story

Calling Christ's People Together *(10 minutes)*

1. A brief explanation of the service may be necessary before you begin.
2. Greeting: The grace of the Lord Jesus Christ be with you.

Response: **And also with you.**

Leader: O God, once upon a time you took a lump of clay and fashioned us into your image. On this Ash Wednesday, you remind us of our dependence on you, for we are but ashes and dust given life by your love. Amen.

3. Sing the hymn: "When We are Living" (or another appropriate hymn from your hymnal).

Proclaiming God's Story *(10 minutes)*

Revised Common Lectionary for Ash Wednesday

Cycles A, B, and C: Joel 2:1–2, 12–17 or Isaiah 58:1–12;
Psalm 51:1–18; 2 Corinthians 5:20b—6:10;
Matthew 6:1–6, 16–21

Crafting God's People into God's Story *(20 minutes)*

1. Silent prayer or meditation is appropriate.
2. A lesson is also appropriate at this time—a story about Lent fits here.

3. Invitation to the observance of Lenten discipline (use the text from your denominational book of worship)
4. Thanksgiving over the Ashes

   Almighty God, you have created us out of the dust of the earth.
   Grant that the ashes may be to us a sign of our mortality and penitence,
   So that we may remember that only by your gracious gift are we given
   Everlasting life, through Jesus Christ our Savior. Amen.

5. Imposition of Ashes

   The leader(s) dip a thumb into the ash container, making the sign of the cross on the forehead of each person saying: "Remember that you are dust, and to dust you shall return."
6. Normally a confession and pardon would happen here, but if you celebrated the carnival, you have already done this. If not, use your denomination's "Order for Confession and Forgiveness."

Going Out into the World and Living God's Word *(10 minutes)*

1. The sending forth of the people of God.
2. Sing a hymn: "I Surrender All" (or another appropriate hymn).
3. Benediction.
4. Going forth: The people depart in silence.

Additional Ideas

1. Ash Wednesday is an appropriate time to use the "Order for Confession and Forgiveness," if one exists in your denomination. Consult with a pastor for books or an order of service.
2. Eucharist is appropriate at the service of Ash Wednesday.
3. An interesting time to hold worship on Ash Wednesday is early morning so that the people of God can attend school and work marked and sealed with the cross of Christ.

Evaluation Questions to Ponder

How is Lent observed in the congregation? What are some ways to enhance the observance of Lent in the parish?

• SEVEN •

Holy Week

Introduction

PASSION SUNDAY. The Holy Week journey begins on this day, also called Palm Sunday. Holy or Passion Week is a time to remember the events that led up to Jesus' suffering and death on the cross. On Palm Sunday, we carry green palm branches to remember our Lord's entry into Jerusalem. The liturgical color for Palm Sunday is purple, violet, or red.

MAUNDY THURSDAY. Maundy means "command." The word is also translated from John 13:34 in a Latin Vulgate Bible to mean "new commandment." On this day, Jesus and the disciples gathered to celebrate the Passover. Jesus washed the disciples' feet. We remember that we are to live a life of servanthood, just as Jesus did. We share the Eucharist because, on this night, Jesus took bread and said, "Take, eat, this is my body," and took a cup of wine and said, "Drink from it, all of you." The liturgical color of the day is white.

GOOD FRIDAY. Jesus was crucified on this day. We remember the cross on which was hung the salvation of the whole world. We wait in silence to celebrate the mystery of our redemption. The liturgical color of the day is black.

In the Roman Catholic Church, there is also the recognition of Holy Saturday, which is the day that Christ descended to the dead, bringing them the good news of his resurrection. Starting with Maundy Thursday in the evening until the Easter vigil, the three days are commonly referred to as the TRIDUUM.

Educator's Notes

THEME OF THE DAY: Remembering the events of Palm Sunday, Maundy Thursday, Good Friday, Holy Saturday, and the Easter vigil that led to Jesus' suffering and death on a cross, which was the way to resurrection.

PRACTICE OF THE DAY: Participating in the acting out of Holy Week events. By doing so prior to Holy Week (strongly suggested), we prepare for Holy Week worship and Jesus' resurrection on Easter Sunday.

Materials Needed

BACKGROUND AND PREPARATION FOR A WALK THROUGH HOLY WEEK

The idea for a Holy Week prayer walk is taken from Gretchen Wolff Pritchard's *Offering the Gospel to Children* (Cambridge, Mass.: Cowley Publications, 1992).

LOCATION OF PRAYER WALK. The walk begins with a series of introductory activities in a fellowship hall or large open space. Movement to various stations is very effective. The sanctuary is suggested for the Last Supper and foot washing, but other arrangements can work as well. A "tomb" area may be created in a dark stairwell or small room without window light.

Leadership. A variety of adult and youth readers may be assigned the Scripture readings. One person may wish to assume the role of Jesus and lead in the washing of feet and reading in the tomb. Another leader may be responsible for the crafts.

Crafts. Many craft catalogs contain appropriate Lenten crafts. Some suggestions for the prayer walk craft time are to weave small crosses out of palm branches or plant a flowering bedding plant in a small container to represent the coming resurrection.

Music Suggestions. Use recorded music on cassette tape or a single flute, recorder, or guitar to accompany singing. Hymns: "Jesus Remember Me" (Taize), "Lord of the Dance" (Shaker Tune), "Were You There?" (Spiritual).

Materials for Prayer Walk

- A variety of Passover foods (prepared in advance): matzo crackers, olives, herbs, dates, water.
- Palm branches, any size.
- Basin of water, towel (may wish to arrange more than one foot washing station).
- Large wooden cross to be carried by participants. Can be constructed in advance from wooden beams, plywood, or tree branches. Size can vary, depending on the size and shape of your group.

- Candles, matches.
- Craft supplies.
- Story Suggestion: Angela Elwell Hunt, *A Tale of Three Trees: A Traditional Folktale* (Oxford, Eng.; Batavia, Ill.: Lion Publications, 1989).

Practicing the Story

Calling Christ's People Together *(10 minutes)*

Gathering activity: Tear apart palm branches in preparation for the walk. Make nametags for participants to wear. Read the story *A Tale of Three Trees.*

Prayer:

God, you sent your son to the world. Your son walked among us, ate with us, and befriended the least likely people, teaching us a new way of life. He walked with a cross on his back to the place of his death. For us and our sins, he died; through his death, we also arose with him on Easter morn. For the gift of the life of Christ, we thank you, O God. Amen.

Proclaiming God's Story *(10 minutes)*

Revised Common Lectionary for Passion Week

Sunday of the Passion, Palm Sunday

Cycles A, B, and C: Matthew 21:1–11; Mark 11:1–11; or John 12:12–16; Luke 19:28–40

Maundy Thursday

Cycles A, B, and C: Exodus 12:1–4, 11–14; Psalm 116: 1, 10–17; 1 Corinthians 11:23–26; John 13:1–17, 31b–35

Good Friday

Cycles A, B, and C: Isaiah 52:13—53:12; Psalm 22; Hebrews 10:16–25 or Hebrews 4:14–16, 5:7–9; John 18:1—19:42

Lesson Scripture for Prayer Walk

Matthew 21:1–11	Matthew 26:17–30
John 13:1–10	Mark 14:32–42
Mark 15:1–15, 21–39	Mark 15:42–27

Crafting God's People into God's Story *(25–30 minutes)*

1. Prayer Walk begins. At each station, leader reads aloud Matthew 21:1–11. Participants carry palm branches in hands. Repeat together: "Hosanna! The Messiah comes!" Walk to sanctuary continuing to wave palm branches.
2. Foot Washing. Jesus warned his disciples that one of them would betray him. In their eagerness to show their loyalty, the disciples began to quarrel and brag about which of them would be most important and special when Jesus became the King. Then Jesus did something to help them understand how they must live if they were to be his friends. Read John 13:1–10. Participants come forward, water is poured over a bare foot, towel used to dry. Return to place around the table.

3. The Last Supper. Arrive in sanctuary, sit, and scatter palm branches on floor. Scripture: Matthew 26:17–30. Food is in place at prepared table or on floor. Altar candles are lit. Following scripture reading, allow for tasting of Passover foods. Sing hymn: "Jesus, Remember Me" or another appropriate hymn from your hymnal.
4. The Arrest, Trial, Crucifixion

   Scripture: Mark 14:32–42. Gethsemane—Participants pretend to sleep.

   Scripture: Mark 15:1–15. Standing before Pilate—Participants stand and at appropriate verse shout "Crucify Him!"

   Scripture: Mark 15:21–39
5. Procession of the Cross.

   In silence, participants gather around a large wooden cross that is lying on the floor. Placing an arm or hand on the bottom of the cross, lift it and (space permitting) carry the cross in continued silence from chancel area to the back of the sanctuary to the narthex or beyond, if space permits. Participants return the cross to the floor when arriving at destination. Move in continued silence to tomb area.
6. The Burial of Jesus

   Scripture: Mark 15:42–47

   While seated in tomb area, sing the hymn: "Were You There?" (or another appropriate hymn). Candles are carried by adults or left in safe "tomb" area and serve as the only light.

Leader reads: Jesus was buried in a cold, dark tomb. Jesus was dead. The people of Israel expected to wait in silence and darkness until the time when God would come to them to set them free and raise them to new life.

A Jesus figure, or leader reads: Awake, sleepers, and rise from the dead, and Christ will give you light! Listen to these words of Jesus: "Rise from the dead, for I am the life of the dead. Out of love for you, I, your God, became a human being, and came to earth. For your sake, I died on the cross. You were driven out of paradise, and I have come to lead you to heaven. I did not create you to be held prisoner forever. As I have died with you, you shall rise with me. The realm of heaven has been prepared for you from all eternity"(adapted from Ephesians 5: 8–14 and hymn "Awake, O Sleeper," words by F. Bland Tucker).

Sing hymn: "Were You There?"

Last verse: "Were you there when they raised him from the tomb?" Participants exit to fellowship hall and sit in a circle.

Going Out into the World and Living God's Word *(10 minutes)*

1. Discuss the Prayer Walk experience. What was your favorite and least favorite Passover food? How did it feel to have your feet washed? Who is likely to do such a thing for you today? (Your mother, a nurse, best friend?) What was it like in the "tomb"? What new discovery did you make during the Prayer Walk? How shall we, the people of God, remember Jesus this week? Record a list of ideas. Number one on the list should be to

attend Holy Week worship services. Resurrection does not happen without Good Friday! End the discussion and then stand in circle, holding hands, and pray together the Lord's Prayer (also known as the Prayer of Our Savior).

2. Craft-making: Create small crosses out of the palm branches. Weaving two branches together in a braid style works well. Secure braid with a knot or piece of tape. Have other crafts available if desired. Invite participants to write comments about the Prayer Walk on a prepared bulletin board as a way of expressing their experiences. Distribute Holy Week and Easter Week schedule of services to all participants.

Additional Ideas

1. Create a Holy Week banner. Observe signs and symbols of Holy Week on church statues or stained glass windows, if possible. Arrange a field trip to a church with Passion Week pictures or stained glass windows.
2. Arrange for a phone chain for participants during Holy Week to offer prayers and invite people to attend the weekly worship services.

Evaluation Questions to Ponder

Think about the questions in "Going Out into the World." Was the Prayer Walk helpful in creating the experiences of Holy Week? How can the Prayer Walk be improved? Careful thought should be considered when selecting an appropriate time for the prayer walk. It could be used as a retreat experience or during Sunday school or catechesis hour or held on the Saturday before Palm Sunday. Was the walk accessible to everyone, especially those who have difficulty moving?

• EIGHT •

Easter

Introduction

The celebration of the Feast of the Resurrection is one of the oldest festivals of the Christian church. Easter is the first Sunday after the first full moon following the vernal equinox (the first day of spring). The Easter season begins on the eve of Easter and ends on the eve of Pentecost, fifty days later. Easter is the most important day of the church year. The resurrection is the cornerstone of the Christian faith. The early church called Easter "Pascha," a word derived from the Hebrew word for Passover. The liturgical color for Easter Day and the Easter season is white.

Educator's Notes

THEME OF THE DAY: Christ is truly risen! Thanks be to God! We celebrate the resurrection of Jesus Christ.

PRACTICE OF THE DAY: Learn the early Easter greeting: "Christ is risen! Christ is risen, indeed! Thanks be to God!" Learn about the Paschal Candle and how it is used in worship. Create Easter symbols and signs of celebration.

Easter celebrations should take place during the Easter season and not during the days before Resurrection Sunday. The following activities may be done on Easter Sunday or any other day following the day we celebrate Christ's resurrection.

Materials Needed

- Craft supplies: crayons, markers, scissors, glue, stapler, glitter in gold and silver.
- Floral wire: enough for creating individual circles of beads approx. 6" in diameter.
- Gold beads to be strung on the floral wire circle.
- A Paschal candle or picture of one if none is available.
- Hymnbooks or song sheets prepared ahead of time.

Practicing the Story

Calling Christ's People Together *(10 minutes)*

1. "Blessed be the God and Father of our Lord Jesus Christ! By his great mercy he has given us new birth into a living hope through the resurrection of Jesus Christ from the dead" (1 Peter 1:3).
2. Sing together Easter hymns of praise and thanksgiving. Use your denomination hymnbook or select in advance hymns and songs reproduced on a song sheet. If no accompanist is available, use taped music to accompany.

   Hymn suggestions:

   "Jesus Christ Is Risen Today." Text: Latin Carol, Charles Wesley, Lyra Davidica. Tune: "Easter Hymn."

   "Now the Green Blade Rises." Text: John M.C. Crum. Tune: "Noel Nouvelet."

"Alleluia, Alleluia, Give Thanks." Text: Donald Fishel. Tune: "Alleluia No. 1."

"Halleluya." Text: South African. Tune: "South African, 1984."

3. The Litany of Celebration (read responsively by whole line)

   Give thanks to the Lord for God is good,
   God's love endures forever.
   I called to the Lord in my distress.
   The Lord answers and frees us.
   The stone that the builders rejected
   Has become the cornerstone.
   This day was made by God,
   We rejoice and are glad.
   Let us go forward in procession with branches.
   You are my God,
   We thank you.
   We praise you, O God.
   Give thanks to the Lord,
   God's love endures forever. (Psalm 118)

Proclaiming God's Story

Revised Common Lectionary for Easter Day

Cycle A: Acts 10:34–43 or Jeremiah 31:1–6
Psalm 118:1–2, 14–24
Colossians 3:1–4 or Acts 10:34–43
John 20:1–18 or Matthew 28:1–10

Cycle B: Acts 10:34–43 or Isaiah 25:6–9
Psalm 118:1–2, 14–24

1 Corinthians 15:1–11 or Acts 10:34–43
John 20:1–18 or Mark 16:1–8

Cycle C: Acts 10:34–43 or Isaiah 65:17–25
Psalm 118:1–2, 14–24
1 Corinthians 15:19–26 or Acts 10:34–43
John 20:1–18 or Luke 24:1–12

Lesson focus: Choose a gospel account of the resurrection to read for the group.

Crafting God's People into God's Story *(20 minutes)*

1. Practice the Easter Greeting. In the early centuries, the faithful embraced each other with the words *"Surrexit Dominus vere"*—"Christ is truly risen!" The correct response was *"Deo gratias"*—"Thanks be to God!"[1] Have the gathered community practice the greeting in Latin and in English as a group, and then go around the room greeting and meeting other members of the body of the risen Christ.
2. Present a Paschal candle to the people (if it is your tradition to use one in worship, bring it carefully from the sanctuary). The Paschal or Easter candle burns during worship from the time of the Easter Vigil (the night before Easter) to Ascension Day, forty days later. The Paschal candle represents the light of Christ, symbolizing Jesus as light of the world, who has forever conquered the dark night of sin.

   Symbols on the candle may be the first and last letters of the Greek alphabet, the alpha and the omega, representing the beginning and the end. The cross on the candle represents Christ; red nails symbolize the wounds Jesus received on the cross. Often the date of the current year is printed on the sides of the cross. The Paschal candle is also lit during the year at baptisms. It can be displayed in the front of the church or near the baptismal font.

Present this brief history of the candle. Allow for questions. Paschal candles are generally not something for home use as are the candles and wreaths of Advent.

3. The following list contains small arts and crafts for the people of God to create in celebration of the resurrection. The theme is the butterfly, a sign of new life and resurrection. Choose from the list below, or create your own butterfly craft.

   - Flying Butterfly. Using floral wire, make a small circle approx. 6" in diameter. String small gold craft beads along the wire so that the result is a circle containing gold beads. Leave the top open to attach a butterfly. Create a butterfly pattern, or use a pre-made butterfly from a craft store to float suspended in the middle of the small circle. The butterfly should be no bigger than 1–2". If making your own butterfly, use any craft materials available to make one out of paper or cardboard. Decorate the butterfly. Attach a small string to the top of the butterfly and attach the string to the top wire of the gold beaded circle. Close the circle by twisting the wire. The butterfly will fly suspended inside the open bead circle. This butterfly creation is a chrismon pattern that can be hung on a chrismon tree at Christmas.

- Butterfly Book. Trace butterfly patterns (made in advance) onto construction paper. Create a small book (any size) using the construction paper as a cover and place inside it several sheets of white drawing paper. Staple the pages together to form a book. Draw picture of the Easter story on the pages or write Easter Bible verses. Continue to use the book as a journal during the Easter season.
- Butterfly Stones. Collect stones of several shapes and sizes, small enough to fit in the palm of one's hand. Paint a symbol of Easter on the stone, like a butterfly, or an egg, an empty cross, a flower. Gather the decorated stones and choose the following:
  a. Give away the stone as a decoration to a family member or friend.
  b. Place a small cross in the middle of a table. Gather all the stones together in a circle around the cross when the painted stones are completed. Say a prayer around the stones, or sing or hum one of the Easter hymns as a closing activity.
  c. Take a photograph, if possible, of this beautiful illustration of Easter hope.

Going Out into the World and Living God's Word *(10 minutes)*

1. Gather the people together for more singing, if desired.
2. Join hands in praying the Lord's prayer (The Prayer of Our Savior) as a group.
3. Practice the Easter greeting: "He is truly risen! Thanks be to God!" Depart in joy and peace to serve the risen Lord.

Additional Ideas

1. Balloons of many colors make wonderful Easter celebration signs. Place helium-filled balloons on car antennas in the church parking lot prior to leaving the activity.
2. Create a banner with the word "Alleluia!" written on it. Design and craft an Easter banner to be used in worship during Easter season.
3. Learn an "Easter alphabet" in another language (Greek perhaps); learn to spell or speak the word "Alleluia" in different languages.

Evaluation Questions to Ponder

1. How is the celebration of Easter continued in the home? The giving of Easter baskets is part of the secular custom. How is the Resurrection brought home?
2. The custom of Easter-egg coloring has its origin in pagan culture but is often brought into the church because of the symbolic meaning of the egg as a symbol of life and renewal, such as Easter eggs from the Ukraine. What other symbols are there?
3. Did the activities contribute to a deeper understanding of worship rituals?

Resources

1. Catalogs from the S & S Craft Supply Company; P.O. Box 513; Colchester, Connecticut 06415-0517, that contain Christian crafts.
2. Pritchard, Gretchen Wolff. *Offering the Gospel to Children.* Cambridge, Mass.: Cowley Publications, 1992.

• NINE •

Ascension

Introduction

The Feast of the Ascension is celebrated forty days after Easter Sunday. On this day, we remember the resurrection and ascension of Jesus Christ into heaven. It is a time to remember that Jesus promised to be with us in witness and mission. The Lord commissioned his apostles to preach the gospel to all nations (Acts 1:9). We celebrate the mystery of Christ's ascension and his glory in heaven. Saint Gregory of Nyssa wrote in a sermon, "The Ascension of Christ is the consummation and fulfillment of all other feasts and the happy conclusion of the earthly sojourn of Jesus Christ."[1]

The celebration of the Feast of Ascension has its origin in very ancient times. In the first three centuries, it was included in the Feast of Pentecost. By the end of the fourth century, Ascension became a separate celebration. Various church traditions celebrated the day with Ascension plays, cross bearing in an Ascension procession, and, of course, special worship celebrations. The liturgical color for Ascension Day is white.

Educator's Notes

Theme of the Day: Jesus' ascension into heavenly glory, a time of celebration and joy, which reflects the hope in our resurrection and ascension. We are called to be his witness in the world.

Practice of the Day: Memorize a scripture verse. Share it with one other person. Make "crowns of glory" that serve as reminders of Jesus and our future glory in him.

Materials Needed

- A crown for a king. Purchase at a party or costume store or make one using cardboard decorated with gold and silver materials.
- Chicken wire cut into the shape of crowns—enough for a large group to make individual crowns. Attach wire together to form a crown circle, carefully bending sharp edges inward to avoid stick points.
- Gold material from a fabric store—enough to cover the crowns.
- Fabric glue and regular glue to attach fabric to crowns.
- Staplers to assist in attaching the fabric to crowns.
- Jewels and beads. Obtain fake jewels and beads from a fabric or craft store to be used as decorations for the crown.
- Hymn: "Crown Him with Many Crowns" on tape or from a hymnbook played by accompanist.

- White 3 x 5 index cards.
- Markers, crayons.
- Masking tape, thumbtacks.
- Wipe board, chalkboard, or writing board of some kind.

Practicing t he Story

Calling Christ's People Together *(10 minutes)*

1. Begin with singing the hymn, "Crown Him with Many Crowns." Text: Matthew Bridges. Tune: Diademata, George J. Elvey. Gather around the display crown and talk about what kind of "equipment" an earthly monarch requires, such as a crown, a scepter, a throne, and a kingdom. Discuss how Jesus on earth did not require these things to save us from our sins. His offering was himself. Explain the meaning of Ascension Day (see introduction). Read Acts 1:1–11.
2. Prayer for the Day.

   With awe and wonder, we pray this prayer of thanksgiving to you, O God, for the word who leapt down to show us your love. In the rising ascension of your son, our prayers of faith, hope, and love arises as well. Amen.

Proclaiming God's Story *(10 minutes)*

Revised Common Lectionary for Ascension Day

Cycles A, B, and C: Acts 1:1–11; Psalm 47; Ephesians 1:15–23; Luke 24:44–53

Lesson Focus: Acts 1:8; Luke 24:45–49

Read the "Lesson Focus" passages. What is the task set before the disciples? The answer is that they should be witnesses to the life, death, resurrection, and ascension of Jesus Christ. Write on a large poster, wipe board, or chalkboard: "You are witnesses of these things—Luke 24:48."

Crafting God's People into God's Story *(20 minutes)*

1. Create crowns of glory. Distribute previously cut chicken wire. Cover with gold materials or other cloth that shines. Attach the jewels or beads to crown with glue. Set crown aside to dry.
2. On 3 x 5 index cards, using markers or crayons, write the sentence that appears on the board: "You are witness to these things—Luke 24:48." Using tape or thumbtacks, walk around the church building and attach cards on doors, bulletin boards, and Sunday school classrooms. Careful instruction and supervision is required so that the cards may be placed in appropriate places.
3. Gather the large group back together. Explain the following, using these words or other appropriate text:

"Today is the fortieth day of Eastertide. We celebrate the ascension of Jesus to divine glory. We do not see Jesus, but he is still with us. Perhaps we do see Jesus whenever we look at another person. Jesus is as close to us as we are to each other. All of us are on our journey home to glory. Let the crowns you have made be a reminder of our future glory with God. We are also called to be witnesses to the life, death, resurrection and ascension of our Lord. We are not to stand around waiting for visions of heaven. We are to see Jesus in others. How can we do this?"[3] Allow the group to brainstorm ideas. You may want to make a list on the wipe board.

4. Say aloud: "You are witnesses of these things. May the risen and ascended Lord Jesus stay close to our hearts and minds so that we can live in his light, walk in his ways, and be witnesses to his love."

5. Practice as a group saying the above witness sentences several times in unison. Commit the sentence text to memory and use it in prayer.

Going Out into the World and Living God's Word *(10 minutes)*

1. Close with prayer petitions from the gathered people. After each petition, the body should respond "Sovereign of glory, hear our prayer."
2. Formal prayer:

   As Christ ascends to you, O God, we await with excitement and joy the Holy Spirit. Come, Holy Spirit! Descend to earth and enter our daily lives! Amen.

Additional Ideas

1. Look in advance for several good Ascension hymns to teach the people. Some suggestions are:

   "Lord, You Give the Great Commission." Text: Jeffery Rowthorn. Tune: "Abbot's Leigh."

   "Alleluia! Sing to Jesus." Text: William C. Dix. Tune: "Hyfrydol."

2. Give decorated crowns to members of the congregation who were not present for the Ascension celebration. Be witnesses to the Ascension story by telling the story as you present the crown.

Evaluation Questions to Ponder

1. Do the people understand the concept of "witness"? Is the scripture text clear in meaning? Be sure to discuss the interpretations of the Ascension story and the Luke text.
2. The crown of glory is also seen again at the Reign of Christ Sunday at the end of the church year. Bringing and wearing the Ascension crowns to worship on the Reign of Christ Sunday might serve as a connection between the two feast days.
3. How does the congregation support witnessing? Perhaps a gathering of the people periodically to talk about witness moments would be helpful.

• TEN •

Pentecost

Introduction

Pentecost is commonly observed as the day that the church was blessed with the Holy Spirit in the belief that the church's birthday is the birth of the Christ child. In Acts 2:1–4, we read that the Holy Spirit came upon the disciples of Jesus in the form of tongues, "as of fire, appeared among them, and a tongue rested on each of them. All of them were filled with the Holy Spirit and began to speak in other languages, as the Spirit gave them ability."

Pentecost is held on the seventh Sunday after Easter. "Pentecost" is the word "fifty" used by Greek-speaking Jews, as in the fifty days after Easter.

In England, Pentecost is usually called "Whitsuntide," or white-Sunday. It is a day for baptism, when new Christians often wear white robes, which may be the reason for the name "Whitsuntide." Other churches hold confirmation on this day. The liturgical color for Pentecost is red. The vestments for Pentecost are red, representing the flame of fire that appeared to the unsuspecting believers in the early church.

Educator's Notes

THEME OF THE DAY: Celebration of the Holy Spirit coming upon and breathing life into the church like a rush of wind.

PRACTICE OF THE DAY: Share with another person the name and story of the first person who shared Jesus Christ with them. Each Christian knows Jesus Christ because someone shared or nurtured them in the name of Jesus Christ as inspired by the Holy Spirit.

Materials Needed

- Red balloons, either filled with helium or ready to blow up with air.
- A red birthday cake with white icing, or white birthday cake with red icing, as a way to signify that we are "celebrating" a most important event in the life of the church.
- A large branch from a tree or bush with some leaves on it. This will be the Name Tree.
- Masking or scotch tape.
- Strips of paper or 3 x 5 cards with John 3:16 printed on the paper or card, with the words in different languages from different countries like German, French, Spanish, or Korean.
- A report or presentation from the missionary supported by the church. Invite former missionaries or groups like the Heifer Project to show ways that the church meets the needs of people far away from the world that we know. You may want a world map in the room to show

where people are coming from in their missionary work or where the church currently has missionaries they support.

- Small, portable fans to set around the room to blow bubbles.
- Red scarves or strips of cloth or red streamers to hang around the room as ornaments.
- Bubbles in containers of children's bubbles or a similar mixture for bubbles and utensils for blowing bubbles. You may choose to have the area where the bubbles will be blown covered with a plastic drop cloth to protect the floor.
- Song, "They Will Know We Are Christians by Our Love," or another appropriate song.

Practicing the Story

Calling Christ's People Together *(10 minutes)*

1. Prepare the fellowship area with red balloons taped to the walls. If helium filled, have balloons ready to be given to people as they arrive. Take red streamers and suspend them from the ceiling, adorning the walls and windows of the room.
2. Bubbles: Someplace in the fellowship area, have bubbles blown by those who want to. Bubbles can be bought at a toy or party store. Some recipe books contain bubble recipes, sometimes found in the back. For homemade bubbles, have enough bubble wands available.

3. Gather people together to sing the song, "They Will Know We Are Christians by Our Love" containing the verse: "We are one in the spirit, we are one in the Lord." This song can be sung *a cappella* or with accompaniment. If possible, have someone use American Sign Language (ASL) to accompany the song.

Proclaiming God's Story *(10 minutes)*

Revised Common Lectionary Reading for Pentecost

Cycle A: Numbers 11:24–30; Psalm 104:24–34, 35b; Acts 2:1–21; John 20:19–23

Cycle B: Ezekiel 37:1–14; Psalm 104:24–34, 35b; Acts 2:1–21; John 15:26–27, 16:4b–15

Cycle C: Genesis 11:1–9; Psalm 104:24–34, 35b; Acts 2:1–21; John 14:8–17

The primary story to be heard in this lesson is from Acts 2:1–21, which tells of the coming of the Holy Spirit, as well as Peter addressing the crowd.

In response to the reading of Acts 2, invite the people to join in the following litany for Pentecost.

Leader: The Holy Spirit is upon us. Alleluia!

People: Come, Holy Spirit.

Leader: The Holy Spirit brings wisdom and knowledge of God.

People: Come, Holy Spirit.

Leader: The Holy Spirit instills charity of heart.

People: **Come, Holy Spirit.**

Leader: The Holy Spirit illuminates the truth.

People: **Come, Holy Spirit.**

Leader: The Holy Spirit enlivens the faithful.

People: **Come, Holy Spirit.**

Leader: The Holy Spirit walks over us with grace.

People: **Come, Holy Spirit.**

Leader: The Holy Spirit nourishes hope.

People: **Come, Holy Spirit.**

Leader: The Holy Spirit inspires us to pray, to lead a life that is Christ-centered and glorifies God.

People: **Come, Holy Spirit.**

Leader: We pray to you, O Spirit of God, to heal our wounded spirits. Blow upon the embers of faith and enlighten us in all the ways you call us and are among us. Amen.

Crafting God's People into God's Story *(20 minutes)*

1. Having asked the Holy Spirit to "rain upon our dry and dusty lives," it is time to hear and receive how God's spirit has brought forth hope in lands and among people who are unlike us. Here, let people who are missionaries, or who represent the mission work of the church, share an anecdote or story from their work. If they have a slide show or video, present it at this time. Think about how much we are still like the first dis-

ciples who spoke different languages, according to the gift of languages bestowed by the Holy Spirit.

2. Name Tree: To demonstrate how God's spirit reaches us at home as well as abroad, have everyone write down on a slip of paper one person who taught them about Jesus Christ. It could be a parent, another family member, a pastor, a teacher, a youth minister, or someone outside the congregation or parish where one attends. Share the name of that person and an anecdote about that person in a small group or with one other person.

   After each person has shared who the person is who shared Jesus Christ with them, have them tape the name of that person on the tree branch, the Name Tree. This tree branch may be moved into the sanctuary as a reminder of all the people whose lives made marks upon other people's lives.

Going Out into the World and Living God's Word *(5 minutes)*

1. Have everyone gather together in a large circle. Read the prophecy of Joel in Acts 2:17–21.
2. Since God's spirit has called on us to prophecy and dream dreams, begin a chorus of people reading John 3:16: "For God so loved the world that he gave his only son, so that everyone who believes in him may not perish but may have eternal life" from the strips of paper made with the passage in different languages. Begin with English, and then have the other languages read so that they slightly overlap one another as each person reads the passage out loud.

3. At the conclusion of the reading identified above, sing together, "They Will Know We Are Christians by Our Love," holding hands and standing together.
4. Enjoy the red birthday cake to celebrate the gifts of the Holy Spirit.

Additional Ideas

1. An Offering of Letters. Find the addresses and names of the missionaries that the congregation supports and encourage the participants to write a letter to one of them. Have the children send pictures.
2. Other Missionaries. Include representatives of the Heifer Project or, perhaps, even Habitat for Humanity to talk about their foreign mission work. Contact the denomination or church's board of missions as well. Invite them to come to the church and present a program.

Evaluation Questions to Ponder

1. Did the people identify or learn something new about a mission project supported by the church?
2. In listening to people read the different languages for John 3:16, what did people hear? Could people understand the different languages or were they just a jumble of words?
3. Could people identify at least one person who shared Jesus Christ with them? Who was that person?

• ELEVEN •

Trinity Sunday

Introduction

Trinity Sunday is the first Sunday after Pentecost and is part of the Pentecost season. Trinity Sunday honors the mystery of the Holy Trinity: God the Father, God the Son, and God the Holy Spirit. The liturgical color for the day is white or green.

The word trinity comes from two words: "tri" and "unity," which means "three united" or "three in one," and has to do with the one God who comes to us in three unique persons. This does not mean there are three Gods. There is one God who reveals Godself to us as father, son, and Holy Spirit.

The Festival of the Holy Trinity was begun by Bishop Stephen of Liege (903–920) and was observed in the Western church. The festival focus was not only the doctrine of the trinity, but a celebration of the work of salvation accomplished from the father, through the son, and in the Holy Spirit.

Educator Notes

THEME OF THE DAY: Who is God? God is three in one: Father, Son, Holy Spirit. God made us, loves us, and is staying with us always.

PRACTICE OF THE DAY: Learn the words of the Apostolic Greeting found in 2 Corinthians 13:13 and share with someone.

Materials Needed

- Tinkertoys or other toy building materials (Legos, foam blocks, and so forth).
- Cardstock paper, any size, in a variety of colors.
- Premixed tempera paint and brushes, any size.
- Apples, enough for everyone to have two.
- Knives to cut open apples.
- Paper towels for clean up.
- Cassette tape player.
- Music: "How Majestic Is Your Name," by Michael W. Smith, or other appropriate musical selection.
- Access to clover or similar foliage that contains three or more leaves (artificial leaves acceptable).
- Bananas and kiwis.
- Optional: A three-legged stool.

Practicing the Story

Calling Christ's People Together *(10 minutes)*

1. Tinkertoy Experiment: Divide a large group into groups of five or less. Groups are given building-toys material (Tinkertoys or other material). The object is to build a three-legged stool. Each group will share the results. If a three-legged stool is available, use it as a model for building. Focus: There are three legs, but one stool. Take away one leg, the stool is less than whole. Trinity Sunday reminds us that the richness of the being of God comes as three persons in one being: Father, Son, and Holy Spirit.
2. Prayer: Holy, holy, holy is the Lord of hosts; the whole earth is full of his glory (Isaiah 6:3). Bless your gathered people with your unending love as we praise and pray in the name of the Father, Son, and Holy Spirit. Amen.

Proclaiming God's Story *(25 minutes)*

Revised Common Lectionary for Trinity Sunday

Cycle A: Genesis 1:1–2; Psalm 8; 2 Corinthians 13:11–13; Matthew 28:16–20

Cycle B: Isaiah 6:1–8; Psalm 29; Romans 8:12–17; John 3:1–17

Cycle C: Proverbs 8:1–4, 22–31; Psalm 8; Romans 5:1–5; John 16:12–15

Lesson Focus—Cycle A

1. Psalm 8: Read the text.

   Focus: the richness of God's being in words majestic (vv. 1, 9), honored (v. 5), caring (v. 4)

   Music: "How Majestic Is Your Name"

   Create a simple dance or body movement to perform with music.

Example: Divide people into groups of 4. Form a circle. Practice the following steps:

   Four steps forward, four steps back (repeat)

   Turn right, walk eight steps forward

   Turn left, walk eight steps forward

   Face in, raise arms up towards sky

   Face in, lower arms to sides, palms up

   Practice and perform.

2. 2 Corinthians 13:11–13: Read and review the text.

   Focus: The word Trinity is not used in the Christian Scriptures, but Father, Son, and Holy Spirit appear in many places such as 2 Corinthians. Our God is three persons in one being.

3. Activity—Apple Prints: One apple per person. Using a knife, cut the apple in half and observe the contents. Three parts: seed, fruit, skin. One whole apple is on the outside; three distinct parts are on the inside. The apple can remind us of the Trinity.

   Dip half of the apple in premixed paint colors and make apple prints on cardstock paper. Create own print design with apples to remember God as three in one.

When print is finished, invite participants to write the following verse on their artwork: God the Father, God the Son, God the Holy Spirit: three in one.

Crafting God's People into God's Story *(5 minutes)*

Review the theme of the day. God made us, loves us, and stays with us. He greets us each day. Practice the Apostolic Greeting in 2 Corinthians 13:13 and memorize it.

If the Apostolic Greeting is used in liturgical worship, review where and when it is used. It is not understood as a blessing, but as a Trinitarian doxology and prayerful greeting. Greet one another with the words.

Going Out Into the World and Living God's Word *(10 minutes)*

Story: It is a mystery how God is three persons in one, and it is difficult to explain. In the church, long ago, there was a man known as St. Patrick of Ireland. The pagans asked Patrick to prove that the Trinity is three persons but still one being. St. Patrick picked up a shamrock leaf. Holding it up, he asked whether he held one leaf or three. The pagans were unable to decide. St. Patrick told them that if they could not explain a simple mystery as the shamrock, how could they hope to understand a mystery so profound as Trinity Sunday?

Read the Great Commission from Matthew 28:19. Give everyone a whole apple (or a banana or kiwi) to take home, as well as the finished apple prints. When the people gather for worship again, encourage them to listen for the Apostolic Greeting.

Additional Ideas

1. Go outside and find a three-leaf clover (or use an artificial one) and use to illustrate the St. Patrick story.
2. Study the various symbols for Trinity Sunday: a shamrock, three circles of equal size interwoven, an equilateral triangle (all sides and angles equal). Create these symbols in art or movement. Symbols are another way to express a profound mystery.
3. Instead of the choreographed dance, have groups create their own steps or movement. Look at some of the confessions and creeds of the church, like the Apostles' Creed, the Nicene Creed, and Athanasian Creed. Focus on the history of the doctrine of the Trinity. Where are the creeds used in church? Where or how is the Trinity mentioned?

Evaluation Questions to Ponder

1. How do you explain a mystery such as the Trinity?
2. What signs or symbols in everyday existence suggest a three-in-one idea?
3. In what ways can the Apostolic Greeting or the Trinitarian language be practiced daily?
4. Which church festivals focus on Jesus? on God the Father? on the Holy Spirit?
5. Find scripture references of Jesus talking with his parent.

Resource

W. Ellwood Post. *Saints, Signs, and Symbols* (New York: Morehouse-Barlow, 1974).

• TWELVE •

All Hallows' Eve and All Saints' Day

Introduction

All Hallows' Eve, All Saints' Day, and All Souls' Day all correspond to All Saints' Day.

All Hallows' Eve, or Halloween, is the evening before All Saints' Day. It is a day first celebrated by the ancient Celts, who called it Samhain (pronounced *sa-oo-en*). The eve of Samhain marked the end of the old year, sweeping out the old and dead, and Samhain was the celebration of the new year. It is the time of the year when the separation between the world of the living and the dead is thin and divination is possible.

In America, Halloween is a time for children to dress up as ghosts and monsters shouting "trick or treat." Some understand that the children in costume represent the dead ancestors and other supernatural beings, and the shout "trick or treat" demands that they be bribed with a treat to keep from playing a trick.

October 31 is also Reformation Day for Lutherans. On this day in 1517, Martin Luther nailed his ninety-five theses on the church door in Wittenberg, Germany, proposing radical changes in the Roman Catholic Church due to what he considered doctrinal error.

All Saints' Day, November 1, can be traced back to the sixth century when, in 835 C.E., Pope Gregory the First's policy of toleration for pagan traditions, like Samhain Eve, was combined with celebrations of the martyrs and other saints of the church.

All Souls' Day, November 2, is the day that Christians pray for the dead, honoring their ancestors by visiting the graves of relatives. It is observed by decorating a grave and lighting a candle, as a remembrance of the dead.[1]

Educator's Notes

THEME OF THE DAY: Remembering the communion of saints and the martyrs of the Christian faith.

PRACTICE OF THE DAY: Remembering, while learning about, the life of one "saint" in the church.

This activity can be practiced either on All Hallows' Eve, All Saints' Day, or All Souls' Day, as the main focus will be on the lives and witness of the "communion of saints."

Who is a saint? Basil Hume, Archbishop of Westminster, perhaps said it best when he said that Christian saints are "the heroic men and women described and speculated upon (who) have bequeathed to us an inspiration that transcends ordinary history . . . for this generation seems to be seeking not the letter which kills, but the spirit which awakens."[2] With that, it is assumed that a "saint" is one whose life is an inspiration that transcends our ordinary life.

The liturgical color for All Saints' Day is white.

Materials Needed

- Multicolored construction paper.
- String or yarn, any color.
- Scissors.
- Glue, tape, or stapler.
- Multicolored marking pens, crayons, or markers.
- Bag or box of odds and ends: For example, have some small feathers, small Styrofoam balls, snippets of wrapping paper, pencil sharpener shavings, bottles of glitter, pipe cleaners, twigs or leaves from a tree or bush, and newspaper or magazines for collages.
- Music: Tape and song sheet, "For All the Saints." Either play on musical instrument or have a tape player available.
- Newsprint or butcher paper.
- Book on saints in the church.
- List of names of those who have died during the last year in the life of a congregation or parish.
- Bags of candy.
- Candle and match.

Practicing the Story (*10 minutes*)

Calling Christ's People Together

1. Have large tables set up in the fellowship hall or common meeting area, with newsprint or butcher paper spread out. On each table have bottles of glue, rolls of tape, construction paper, scissors, yarn or string, bags of stuff, and crayons and markers all spread out on the top of the tables.
2. Have a stencil ready to be used as a guide for making masks out of construction paper to be worn over the eyes. Cut out the masks with scissors. These masks are to be of someone who is significant in our life, whose presence makes, or has made, our life in Christ richer. They can be masks that reflect either those who currently make an impression on our lives or have since died and are now members of the communion of saints. On All Hallows' Eve, All Saints' Day, and All Souls' Day, we remember saints who have come before us and lead us still.

At the end of this activity, gather everyone together with their masks on to pray this prayer:

> God of the living, and God of the dead yet who are alive in you, take our well-decorated lives, so that they may be of service unto you. Our memories of those whose lives have shaped ours are coming alive. Blow softly upon the embers as we remember, and are remembered, to the saints, the martyrs, the lives of those women and men whom you have called to your bosom. We pray this in the name of Christ. Amen.

Proclaiming God's Story (*10 minutes*)

<u>Revised Common Lectionary Reading for All Saints' Day</u>

Cycle A: Revelation 7:9–17; Psalm 34:1–10; 1 John 3:1–3; Matthew 5:1–12

Cycle B: Isaiah 25:6–9; Psalm 24; Revelation 21:1–6a; John 11:32–44

Cycle C: Daniel 7:1–3, 15–18; Psalm 149; Ephesians 1:11–2:23; Luke 6:20–31

1. Lesson focus for cycles A and C: Matthew 5:1–12 or Luke 6:20–31 (The Beatitudes). Read aloud these passages, which are both about what characteristics Jesus is calling on Christians to have to be part of the kingdom of heaven. These might sound strange by some, such as those who are poor, or poor of spirit, are blessed more so than those who are wealthy. What does it mean that Christians should be "persecuted for righteousness' sake"? Or that "people revile you and persecute you and utter all kinds of evil against you falsely on my account. Rejoice and be glad, for your reward is great in heaven, for in the same way they persecuted the prophets who were before you" (Matthew 5:10–12)?

   Either in one large group or in smaller groups, have people name a Christian who has taught them one of the characteristics that are called "blessed" by Jesus. List also some characteristics that this person taught us. Such people, who show us these characteristics in practice, are the saints among us or those who have gone before.

2. Lesson focus for cycle B: John 11:32–44. In this passage, Jesus raises his friend Lazarus to life, revealing that his power is the same as the one true God, because no one else but God can raise the dead back to life. It is this same Jesus who performs miracles in our life this day by saving us and making us members of the communion of saints.

   Like the focus for cycles A and C, list the names on newsprint of those Christians, whether they are with us today or not, whom you would consider saints and in whose lives you see Jesus in the life of the church.

Crafting God's People into God's Story *(10 minutes)*

Do one or more of the following activities:

1. Choose a Saint: Using either *Butler's Lives of the Saints* or another book on the life of saints, choose a saint to learn about this day. It could be a saint whose life is celebrated on someone's birthday, or it could be a saint in someone's life. Either read aloud the story of a saint to others in the group or tell them the story of a saint in your life.

   Then make a large button or pin, using the leftover paper and a marking pen, with the name of the saint on the pin or button. Have people mingle and ask one another something about the saint whose name they are wearing.
2. Telling Saints Apart: Each person or group draws a picture or symbol of a saint on newsprint. On the edges

of the paper, or on another sheet, write some of the characteristics or historical anecdotes about the life of the saint. Tape the newsprint up on the wall, encouraging all the people in the room to read the lives of the saints. Or place the newsprint paper down on the floor, as though it is a cemetery, and people could wander around the fellowship area as if they were visiting it.

3. A Time of Remembering: Gather everyone together in a group. Light one large candle, placed in a candleholder, to be passed around the circle of people. Begin by naming the people who have died this year in the life of a congregation or parish, remembering one anecdote or story about each person's life, followed by silence or other memories. Do not rush the activity.

   Each person will be given a turn to tell something "extraordinary" about a rather "ordinary" saint in our lives who has lived the Beatitudes, the Gospel of God. Pass the candle to each person, young and old alike, as each tells a story about a person whose life has made an impression on them. In between each passing of the candle, the group may sing or chant, "Jesus remember me, when you come into your kingdom; Jesus remember me, when you come into your kingdom." Another chant may follow: "Lord, in your mercy," with the response, "Hear our prayer."

   Again, have paper, pens, and pins ready to make a button or pin with the name of the saint in your life who helps you live the Gospel of God.

Going Out into the World and Living God's Word *(10 minutes)*

1. Gather together in a circle to sing, "For All the Saints," accompanied by a musical instrument or by an audiotape.
2. Proclaim that, on this day, we remember those who have died from a specific congregation or parish in the year since the last All Saints' Day and All Souls' Day.
3. Remember in prayer the names of those who have died, and lift up the names of other saints whose lives have made an impression on people as they lived the Beatitudes of Jesus.
4. Ask the people when they leave to wear the button or pin with the saint's name on it all day.

Additional Ideas

1. Visit the grave of a friend, family member, or someone whose life was significant to your life. Take a flower or a candle and spend some time in quiet reflection.
2. Write to or call a saint in your life and tell them why you are communicating with them. Write letters and mail them on this day as one of the activities for the gathered group.

Evaluation Questions to Ponder

1. How are people who have died in the church remembered?
2. What other time can we remember the lives of the saints in the church? the Eucharist?

• THIRTEEN •

The Reign of Christ

Introduction

The Reign of Christ, or Christ the King, Sunday is considered the last Sunday of the Christian year. The liturgical color is white. Christ demands our acknowledgment of him as king, or as ruler of our lives as Christians, and the Reign of Christ Sunday seems an appropriate time to remind us of this fact. Christ the King Sunday was established as an official feast day in 1925 by Pope Pius XI. The underlying theme of this feast was to be a time for Christians to recognize the reign of Christ, to offer up all of their concerns expressed in naming him "king and ruler," and to allow him to accept these concerns as only our sovereign Lord could.

Because The Reign of Christ Sunday and Thanksgiving Day come during the same week in the United States of America, the latter often takes the majority of our planning, while the former tends to slip by almost unnoticed. An alternative to this typical scenario is the "Feast of Thanksgiving for Christ the King," a way to recognize both occasions. The Reign of Christ Sunday falls at a very transitional time in a liturgical year, as it is the last Sunday of the year leading directly into the first Sunday of Advent, the beginning of a new year. This provides educators an excellent opportunity to move towards Advent with the idea of baby Jesus being also the sovereign Christ whom we must hail as ruler.

Educator's Notes

THEME OF THE DAY: Acknowledging Christ as our ruler who reigns over us means having faith in him to lead and to protect us in the ways of his love.

PRACTICE OF THE DAY: Create symbols of "rulership" based on the narratives of the Reign of Christ in and over our lives. At the end of the church year, create a list of blessings in the past year for which we praise God. Create a list of situations Christ has triumphed over in the past year.

This program is designed to follow a feast, be it typical Thanksgiving delicacies or otherwise. The decorations should avoid any of the turkeys, Pilgrims, and so on that we usually associate with Thanksgiving. Rather, they should consist mainly of the colors white and gold, with the possible addition of purple as a color of royalty. The room should be set up in a manner conducive for dividing a group of people into four groups, each having a work area or a table to work on for the following activities.

Materials Needed

- Decorations of any variety, gold and silver if possible, like bunting, crepe paper, streamers or regular balloons and streamers.
- Work areas for each of the four divided groups with a large board, hammer and nails, glue gun, stapler, tape, or other mounting tools.

- Tables set up with a variety of craft materials for use such as paper, glue, scissors, Popsicle sticks, markers, scrap material, and nature items such as leaves, branches, flowers, and so forth.
- Note cards containing directions for activity in "Crafting God's People in God's Story."
- Hymnbooks or song sheets prepared in advance. Accompanist also suggested.
- Bibles for reference.
- Tagboard.

Practicing God's Story

Calling Christ's People Together *(15 minutes)*

1. Begin singing hymns that recognize Christ as our ruler. If a trumpet player is available, use as accompaniment for hymns. Hymn suggestions:

   "All Glory, Laud and Honor," "O Worship the King," "Rejoice, the Lord is King," "At the Name of Jesus," "Crown Him with Many Concerns," "We Will Glorify, Jesus Shall Reign."

You could also play portions of G. F. Handel's *Messiah.*

2. Following the hymn singing, a Psalm response:

Leader:	Make a joyful noise to the Lord, all the earth.
People:	**Worship the Lord with gladness; come into his presence with singing.**
Leader:	Know that the Lord is God.
People:	**It is he that made us and we are his; we are his people, and the sheep of his pasture.**

Leader:	Enter his gates with thanksgiving, and his courts with praise.
People:	**Give thanks to him, bless his name.**
Leader:	For the Lord is good; his steadfast love endures forever,
People:	**And his faithfulness to all generations.**—Psalm 100

3. Time for Prayer. Give thanks to God for the many blessings he has bestowed on our lives and the lives of those in our congregation. Thank him for the gift of Christ who reigns over our lives. Ask God to be with all of us during this event and to reveal himself in the hearts of those present.

Proclaiming God's Story *(10 minutes)*

Revised Common Lectionary Reading for the Reign of Christ

Cycle A: Ezekiel 34:11–16, 20–24; Psalm 95:1–7a; Ephesians 1:15–23; Matthew 25:31–46

Cycle B: Daniel 7:9–10, 13–14; Psalm 93; Revelation 1:4b–8; John 18:33–37

Cycle C: Jeremiah 23:1–6; Psalm 46; Colossians 1:11–20; Luke 23; 33–43

Lesson Focus: Jeremiah 23:1–6; John 10:11–16; Luke 23:33–43; Revelation 19:11–16; John 12:12–15

1. Read aloud the story in John 12:12–15. Option: Have different people read parts for the different characters in the story.
2. A time of explanation will be necessary. Take a moment to clarify the point on the liturgical calendar where the

Reign of Christ falls. Clarify the purpose of the feast for your congregation, that it is a time of thanksgiving to God for providing the reign of Christ.

Crafting God's People into God's Story *(10 minutes)*

1. Divide the large group into four smaller groups. Assign each group to a workplace in the room. Provide each group with a note card of directions for proceeding. The top line of the note card will identify the group as one of the following:

   The Reign of Christ was prophesied in Jeremiah 23:1–6

   Christ the Shepherd, John 10:11–16

   Christ the Servant, Luke 23:33–43

   Christ the Returning Sovereign of Sovereigns, Revelation 19:11–16

   The note cards will have the following directions:

   —Read the scripture assigned to your group.

   —Talk about the type of reign of Christ characterized in the passage read. Think of different words to describe Christ's rulership, reign, or God's dominion.

   —Think of something (or several things) that your group can create from the materials available that will somehow symbolize the type of kingship or reign of Christ you read about. For example, you could create a shield with a coat of arms, or a flag with a crest symbolizing the reign of Christ. You will be mounting these symbols on tagboard in whatever way you choose.

—Take time to create your symbols and design your tagboard.

—Designate a spokesperson (or several) to share with the large group your scripture passage and board. Explain why the particular symbols chosen relate to the type of rulership in your passage.

—List the things to praise God for that show how Christ has reigned during the past Christian year. (For example, other people who have blessed you, situations where Christ has been present, lessons Christ has taught you.)

2. When each group is finished, have everyone return to their original seats. Explain that each group will present their passages and board designs to all the people.
3. When presentations are complete, ask everyone to take a moment in silent prayer, thinking about the different symbols they have seen and thanking God again for his gift of Christ and his reign in our lives.
4. Each group should have a completed list of praises and thanksgivings for Christ. Make sure that the group list is attached to the designs of each group.

Going Out into the World and Living God's Word *(10 minutes)*

1. Move from thanksgiving for all blessings that have been and picture the promise of a bright future with God. Quietly meditate on the anticipation of the Messiah coming in Advent.

2. Sing a final hymn, "Soon and Very Soon" Text: 7. Tune by Andre Crouch or another appropriate song.
3. Display the design boards during Advent to remind the congregation of the baby Jesus' rulership.

Additional Ideas

1. Compare various crowns of monarchs, rulers, kings, and queens. After a historical look at kings and queens and their crowns, bring into the discussion the crown that Jesus wore on earth: the crown of thorns. What does this say about Jesus?
2. Review and seek scripture passages that speak to the question that Jesus asked of Peter: "Who do you say that I am?" The gathered community may also answer the question.

Evaluation Questions to Ponder

1. How are kings or rulers welcomed into a community? Bring into the discussion the Passion story entrance of Jesus into Jerusalem. Look at several Hebrew Scripture kings and their anointed beginnings such as Saul or David.
2. Why is the reign of Christ appropriate as the last Sunday of the Christian year?
3. What kinds of symbols will we use to remember who we are as children of God? What symbol of the reign of Christ?

Notes

CHAPTER 2

1. Karen Bellenir, ed., *Religious Holidays and Calendars: An Encyclopedic Handbook*, 2nd ed. (Detroit, Mich.: Omnigraphics, 1998), 76–77.

CHAPTER 3

1. Gertrud Mueller Nelson, *To Dance with God: Family Ritual and Community Celebration* (New York: Paulist Press, 1986), 117.

CHAPTER 5

1. *Webster's New Collegiate Dictionary*, 3rd. ed. s.v. "transfigure."

2. Inter-Lutheran Commission on Worship, *Lutheran Book of Worship* (Minneapolis, Minn.: Augsburg Fortress Press, 1978), 17.

CHAPTER 6

1. Steve Englehart, *Easter Parade*, (New York: Avon Camelot, 1995), 27–28.

2. Nelson, *To Dance with God*, 133.

3. Ibid., 132.

4. James F. White, *Introduction to Christian Worship* (Nashville, Tenn.: Abingdon, 1980), 61.

CHAPTER 8

1. Franz Xaver Weiser, *Handbook of Christian Feasts and Customs: The Year of the Lord in Liturgy and Folklore* (New York: Harcourt, Brace, 1958), 212.

CHAPTER 9

1. Weiser, *Handbook of Christian Feasts and Customs*, 243.

CHAPTER 12

1. Bellenir, *Religious Holidays and Calendars*, 94–95; 221.

2. Alban Butler (1711–1773), *Butler's Lives of the Saints*, foreword and ed. Michael Walsh (New York: HarperCollins, 1991).

OTHER BOOKS FROM THE PILGRIM PRESS

Resources for the Liturgical Year

DON C. SKINNER

An eloquent, informative, and extremely useful worship resource, this book provides a vast array of prayers, liturgical readings, calls to praise, calls to confession, prayers of praise, and much more.

0-8298-1217-2/paper/240 pages/$16.95

An Improbable Gift of Blessings

Prayers and Affirmations to Nurture the Spirit

MAREN TIRABASSI AND JOAN JORDAN GRANT

Designed for those who use the lectionary as well as those who do not, this resource is a diary of prayer that invites individuals and congregations into an involvement with scripture and community to engage the heart and nurture the spirit.

0-8298-1220-2/paper/176 pages/$15.95

To order these or any other books from The Pilgrim Press call or write:

The Pilgrim Press
700 Prospect Avenue East
Cleveland OH 44115-1100

Phone orders:

800.537.3394 • Fax orders: 216.736.2206
Please include shipping charges of $4.00 for the first book and 75¢ for each additional book.
Or order from our web sites at <www.pilgrimpress.com> and <www.ucpress.com>.

Prices subject to change without notice.